BARBECUE COOKBOOK

Carol Bowen

Hamlyn

London New York Sydney Toronto

Acknowledgements

Front cover photograph by John Lee
Photographs on pages 55, 65, 68, 77, 78, 96, 113, 114
by Christian Délu/PAF International.
Photograph on page 38 by John Lee, courtesy of Tower
Housewares Limited. All other photography by Vic Paris
of Alphaplus Studios, Leatherhead.
Line drawings by Ann Rees and Tony Streek

Published by
The Hamlyn Publishing Group Limited
London New York Sydney Toronto
Astronaut House Feltham Middlesex England

Fifth impression 1982

ISBN 0 600 31463 4

Phototypeset by Tradespools Ltd Frome Somerset
Printed in Italy by New Interlitho S.p.A. - Milan

The following titles are also
available in this series:

Chicken Cookbook
Cocktails and Mixed Drinks
Contact Grill
Cooking with Yogurt
Curry Cookbook
Diabetic Cookbook
Egg and Cheese Cookbook
Fred's Pastry Book
Kitchen Magic
Mighty Mince Cookbook
No Need to Cook Book
Pressure Cookbook
Short Cut Cookbook
Woman and Home Favourite Recipes

CONTENTS

USEFUL FACTS AND FIGURES

Notes on metrication

In this book quantities are given in metric and Imperial measures. Exact conversion from Imperial to metric measures does not usually give very convenient working quantities and so the metric measures have been rounded off into units of 25 grams. The table below shows the recommended equivalents.

Ounces	Approx g to nearest whole figure	Recommended conversion to nearest unit of 25	Ounces	Approx g to nearest whole figure	Recommended conversion to nearest unit of 25
1	28	25	11	312	300
2	57	50	12	340	350
3	85	75	13	368	375
4	113	100	14	396	400
5	142	150	15	425	425
6	170	175	16 (1 lb)	454	450
7	198	200	17	482	475
8	227	225	18	510	500
9	255	250	19	539	550
10	283	275	20 (1¼ lb)	567	575

Note When converting quantities over 20 oz first add the appropriate figures in the centre column, then adjust to the nearest unit of 25. As a general guide, 1 kg (1000 g) equals 2.2 lb or about 2 lb 3 oz. This method of conversion gives good results in nearly all cases, although in certain pastry and cake recipes a more accurate conversion is necessary to produce a balanced recipe.

Liquid measures The millilitre has been used in this book and the following table gives a few examples.

Imperial	Approx ml to nearest whole figure	Recommended ml	Imperial	Approx ml to nearest whole figure	Recommended ml
¼ pint	142	150 ml	1 pint	567	600 ml
½ pint	283	300 ml	1½ pints	851	900 ml
¾ pint	425	450 ml	1¾ pints	992	1000 ml (1 litre)

Spoon measures All spoon measures given in this book are level unless otherwise stated.

Can sizes At present, cans are marked with the exact (usually to the nearest whole number) metric equivalent of the Imperial weight of the contents, so we have followed this practice when giving can sizes.

Flour Either plain or self-raising flour can be used in the recipes unless specified.

Herbs Use fresh unless specified otherwise.

Oven temperatures

The table below gives recommended equivalents.

	°C	°F	Gas Mark		°C	°F	Gas Mark
Very cool	110	225	$\frac{1}{4}$	Moderately hot	190	375	5
	120	250	$\frac{1}{2}$		200	400	6
Cool	140	275	1	Hot	220	425	7
	150	300	2		230	450	8
Moderate	160	325	3	Very hot	240	475	9
	180	350	4				

Notes for American and Australian users

In America the 8-oz measuring cup is used. In Australia metric measures are now used in conjunction with the standard 250-ml measuring cup. The Imperial pint, used in Britain and Australia, is 20 fl oz, while the American pint is 16 fl oz. It is important to remember that the Australian tablespoon differs from both the British and American tablespoons; the table below give a comparison. The British standard tablespoon, which has been used throughout this book, holds 17.7 ml, the American 14.2 ml, and the Australian 20 ml. A teaspoon holds approximately 5 ml in all three countries.

British	American	Australian	British	American	Australian
1 teaspoon	1 teaspoon	1 teaspoon	$3\frac{1}{2}$tablespoons	4 tablespoons	3 tablespoons
1 tablespoon	1 tablespoon	1 tablespoon	4 tablespoons	5 tablespoons	$3\frac{1}{2}$ tablespoons
2 tablespoons	3 tablespoons	2 tablespoons			

An Imperial/American guide to solid and liquid measures

Solid measures

IMPERIAL	AMERICAN
1 lb butter or margarine	2 cups
1 lb flour	4 cups
1 lb granulated or castor sugar	2 cups
1 lb icing sugar	3 cups
8 oz rice	1 cup

Liquid measures

IMPERIAL	AMERICAN
$\frac{1}{4}$ pint liquid	$\frac{2}{3}$ cup liquid
$\frac{1}{2}$ pint	$1\frac{1}{4}$ cups
$\frac{3}{4}$ pint	2 cups
1 pint	$2\frac{1}{2}$ cups
$1\frac{1}{2}$ pints	$3\frac{3}{4}$ cups
2 pints	5 cups ($2\frac{1}{2}$ pints)

Note When making any of the recipes in this book, only follow one set of measures as they are not interchangeable.

American terms

The list below gives some American equivalents or substitutes for terms and ingredients used in this book.

Equipment and terms

BRITISH/AMERICAN	BRITISH/AMERICAN
cling film/saran wrap	mince/grind
cocktail stick/toothpick	mould/mold
flan tin/pie pan	packet/package
foil/aluminum foil	piping bag/pastry bag
greaseproof paper/waxed paper	polythene/plastic
liquidise/blend	top and tail/stem and head

Ingredients

BRITISH/AMERICAN

aubergine/eggplant
bacon rasher/bacon slice
biscuit/cookie or cracker
black grapes/purple grapes
black olives/ripe olives
cauliflower sprigs/cauliflowerets
celery stick/celery stalk
chilli/chili pepper
cooking apple/baking apple
cornflour/cornstarch
courgettes/zucchini
demerara sugar/brown sugar
digestive biscuits/graham crackers
double cream/heavy cream
essence/extract
gelatine/gelatin

BRITISH/AMERICAN

green grapes/white grapes
ham/cured or smoked ham
hard-boiled eggs/hard-cooked eggs
lard/shortening
minced beef/ground beef
peeled prawn/shelled shrimp
root ginger/ginger root
seedless raisins/seeded raisins
single cream/light cream
soft brown sugar/light brown sugar
spring onion/scallion
stock cube/bouillon cube
sweetcorn/corn
tomato purée/tomato paste
unsalted butter/sweet butter
vanilla pod/vanilla bean

In spite of unpredictable weather, there is something irresistibly festive about eating out of doors. Perhaps it is the sight and aroma of food sizzling over a hot barbecue or the alfresco nature of cooking food out of doors instead of in a kitchen that makes the difference. A happy fact since no meal is more fun to prepare.

There is nothing very difficult about preparing meals in the open air, but a certain amount of basic knowledge helps to avoid some of the pitfalls, such as a smoky fire, food charred on the outside yet raw in the middle, and lukewarm drinks. It is hoped that this book will provide an easy guide to choosing and using the various types of barbecue available, managing the fire as well as preparing food for outdoor use. Help on the quantities of food to prepare are all important too, since fresh air sharpens appetites. There are ideas here for simple family meals through to grand parties.

Although relatively new in popularity in this country, millions of people all over the world enjoy the delights of barbecued food. I hope this book will give you all the advice you need to join them. Bon appétit!

Carol Bowen

ALL ABOUT BARBECUES

CHOOSING A BARBECUE

The basics of barbecuing are really quite simple. You will need cooking and serving equipment, fuel and food, and a place to eat. But within that framework the choices are anything but easy.

The barbecue equipment you will find in stores and garden centres ranges from the simple to the sumptuous, so it pays to compare and at first limit purchases to those that are essential. If, after experimenting, you find that your enjoyment of barbecuing merits extra investment, then move up the scale to the fancier equipment. The money invested initially in a small grill will not be wasted; it can still be used as a second barbecue for cooking appetisers and keeping food hot.

From the many types of barbecue on the market you will first have to choose between portable and permanent. If you think you will use your barbecue regularly, and your garden or patio affords the space for it, you might consider a permanent fixture rather than a portable unit, whatever size of barbecue you need. Small ones are very easy to make yourself (see page 15) and larger ones have the advantage that working surfaces and storage spaces can be built in as required, as can warming ovens and other extras.

Whatever type of barbecue you buy, its construction is extremely important. Grills should be made of nickel and chrome-plated steel, with bars close enough together to stop the food falling through. Spits and spit forks should also be of heavy chrome-plated steel and sturdy enough to support heavy weights without bending unduly.

Above all a barbecue must be stable, so check that it does not wobble. Before buying a portable unit with screw-in or telescopic legs, check that they will stay put when the barbebue is erected *and* fully laden.

Check that the grill can be easily lowered or raised and that the mechanism for doing this is easy to grip and made from wood or any other insulating material.

When checking a heavy covered unit make sure the lid is reasonably close fitting. A hood should cover at least 50% of the bowl. A lid that is air tight used in conjunction with an air-vent will allow accurate control of the temperature within the cooking area.

If the barbecue has wheels, check that they are free moving. That models which work on gas or electricity are near an electrical outlet or on an extension cord, or near a stable area for a gas tank to be located. It is also useful to check that large models can be dismantled easily for storage.

Additional folding grills and double grills are useful equipment for handling more delicate food, so check that your barbecue can accommodate extra items of this nature.

Portable barbecues

Hibachi

This is a barbecue that originated in Japan but has proved to be very popular all over the world, especially to the beginner, because of its basic simplicity and low cost. Round or rectangular hibachis are available in two styles, table top or free-standing (which have legs or pedestals), and are usually made from heavy cast black metal. Lightweight versions of the hibachi, made from pressed steel or aluminium, in a variety of colours, are now available.

The surface area of the hibachi is fairly small and will only accommodate up to six people, although new 'double' and 'triple' hibachis will cope with larger quantities.

Hibachis have draught controls in the side or front of the fire-bowl to assist with lighting the fuel and controlling the rate of burning. Choose a model that has a fire-bowl at least 7·5 cm/3 inches deep.

Picnic

Picnic barbecues are small barbecues, usually round in shape, and easily portable. They generally have a 45-cm/18-inch circular revolving grill, although many different styles are available. Some models have a wind shield and few incorporate a spit. They are adequate for up to eight people.

Brazier

The next step up is the brazier or open barbecue. Although similar in many ways to the picnic barbecue, the larger brazier models are more suitable for use in the garden or patio for increased quantities.

The circular grill size of this barbecue ranges from 45–60 cm/18–24 inches. Most models have folding or screw-in legs and the best versions have adjustable grills and wheels. Consider one with an additional work surface or small shelf if you intend to cook for lots of people, or if this is not included look out for a clip-on tray.

Hooded

The basic difference between the hooded barbecue and the brazier is, of course, the hood. The hood fulfils two important functions; it protects food cooking on the grill from the cooling effects of breezes, and it helps to prevent smoke from swirling in the face of the chef and guests. It also provides support and mountings for a spit.

Some hooded barbecues have a warming oven, usually with a door, inside the upper part of the hood. This is useful for keeping plates and cooked food warm. Other variations include folding legs,

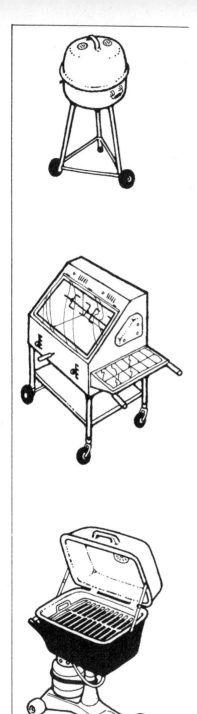

detachable hoods, work shelves and wheels. The hooded barbecue is capable of catering for up to 25 people, as long as the food is not too ambitious.

Kettle

Perhaps the most effective hooded barbecue is the kettle grill. When closed, the hood completely covers the fire-bowl. Most versions are spherical or rect-angular in shape and are made from either cast aluminium or porcelain enamelled steel, and have wheels for easy moving.

The top half of the kettle grill is usually fixed to the lower half by hinges, and when raised the top acts as a windbreak. When the lid is closed, the reflected heat within the dome browns the top of the meat. The deep fire-bowl and the dome-shaped lid have adjustable vents to control the draught. When cooking is completed, both vents can be closed to snuff out live coals.

The kettle grill is considered ideal for barbecuing in windy or breezy places and is excellent for smoking food. Spherical kettle grills are 45–55 cm/18–22 inches in diameter.

Wagon

The wagon grill, as its name suggests, is a large covered barbecue mounted on a wheeled wagon. The main body of the barbecue is usually of a rectangular-box shape but cylindrical models are also available.

Wagon grills are often the most sophisticated of barbecues and may include oven temperature gauges, warming ovens, heat-tempered glass panels in the door and built-in storage cabinets.

Grill areas are large and the distance between the grill and the coals can be adjusted by either raising the grill or lowering the fire pan. Most wagon grills have motorised spits whilst some allow access to the fire by a separate door.

Like the kettle grill, the wagon grill allows efficient heat control, even on wet and windy days, and it can be used to smoke meat and fish. Because of their size they are often confined to patio use. They are not particularly easy to dismantle and it is therefore wise to consider storage before embarking upon purchase.

Gas and electric

For those people who wish to enjoy some of the pleasures of barbecuing without getting involved in the preparation of a charcoal fire, gas and electricity provide the answer.

In both gas and electric barbecues, natural lava rock, or a similar man-made product, is used instead of charcoal. When heated by the gas flame or electric element, the rock emits a radiant heat. The heat level is controlled, just like an oven, by the turn of a knob.

After cooking is completed, the greasy lava rock can be cleaned by placing a piece of aluminium foil loosely on top of the heating element and rock, and turning the control knob to its highest setting. After about ten minutes, most of the grease and impurities in the rocks will have been burnt off.

Both gas and electric barbecues can be used to smoke food, providing, of course, that they have a hood. This is done by placing a small piece of hickory or applewood, or chips of the same, on to the heated rock and then keeping the hood closed.

Most gas barbecues can be adapted for use with either natural or liquid propane bottled gas.

For indoor use, these types have the advantage that their ventilation requirements are little more than those of an ordinary cooker.

Permanent barbecues

Building one's own barbecue can make good sense for those who make barbecuing a regular habit. There are a tremendous variety of permanent barbecues that can be built by an amateur or professional builder, both in and out of doors; but a few simple rules need to be observed for success, particularly in siting an outdoor barbecue.

Indoor barbecues

Probably the best site indoors is in the fireplace. The fireplace itself may be used as the fire-box or a separate fire-box could be built in or built for the fireplace, but make sure when in use that the draught is open.

A barbecue could also be built into a porch at the front or back of the house, in a sheltered position. The barbecue could then be constructed to share the same chimney ducting as the indoor fireplace.

Outdoor barbecues

If space permits, it is not difficult to build a permanent barbecue in the garden. Make sure the site is far enough away from the house so as not to be a fire hazard, yet near enough to make food and drink reinforcements practical. Points to consider are:

Location Choose an attractive place but also one that is practical. If you have a terrace to your house this is often an ideal spot, being within easy reach of the kitchen. Wherever you choose, make sure that it can be well lit and that the area is well-drained and shaded from any strong breezes. Keep well away from trees, shrubs or wooden buildings.

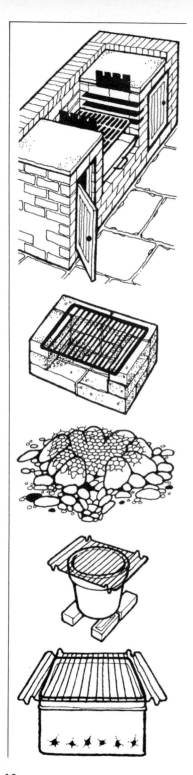

Surrounding area If at all possible consider paving the surrounding area so that guests can easily walk to and from the barbecue. Allow at least 1 metre to the front and sides of a small barbecue and 2 metres or more for a larger barbecue.

Foundations Make sure the barbecue has a solid foundation which extends below the frost line.

Construction Do not make the barbecue too low on the ground, this can be back breaking, but preferably waist height so that it can be easily handled. Grill positions, dampers, draughts and chimneys are all a matter for personal consideration, but varying grill heights will ensure a variety of cooking methods, dampers and draughts will make the fire easier to manage, and a chimney is necessary if you want to burn a great deal of wood. When building remember to leave sufficient room for expansion and contraction of any metal parts, to prevent them from breaking and cracking any surrounding brick work.

Impromptu barbecues

Basically a barbecue is nothing more than a grill on which food can be cooked over a fire-bed of glowing hot coals. Very simple forms of this arrangement can be improvised with a grill pan rack or a double thickness of chicken wire on a large flower pot, an old chrome-plated refrigerator rack on top of a large biscuit tin or over a frame of loose bricks, and so on. To ensure that you have enough draught, raise the plant pot on bricks, punch holes in the biscuit tin or loosely pile the bricks leaving air holes between them.

The beach is an ideal place for a barbecue. You can of course take your own barbecue and fuel to the beach but it is often more fun to improvise. On a sandy beach make a hollow for the fire-bed and dig one or two tunnels into this from the side of the prevailing wind, so that air can feed the fire. A ring of big, dry stones around the edge will serve to support the temporary structure. On a pebbly beach build up a ring of largish stones to surround the fire-bed, again leaving sufficient space for air to feed the fire. Cover over with a piece of chicken wire. Fuel can be in the form of driftwood, but allow to burn down to embers before starting to cook.

Metal coathangers can be used for skewers should you wish to do this kind of cooking.

An old wheelbarrow made of metal can also be used as a barbecue base. Put some large stones in the bottom to even up to a flat surface. Place the fuel on this and top with a grill rack extending over the sides of the wheelbarrow. This could be an oven shelf, cake rack or old refrigerator shelf; if made of metal. You can also make an impromptu brick barbecue for

your garden. Form a rectangle of bricks, allowing three bricks down each side of the barbecue and four at the back and front. Build the bricks three high, leaving an air hole at the back and front. Top with an improvised grid and fill up with gravel and charcoal briquets to come to the top of the bricks.

Fuel

Charcoal is far and away the most popular form of household barbecue fuel today, but wood can be used for permanent fire-sites and for impromptu barbecues. An exception being a small special barbecue that uses no more than a few sheets of newspaper as its fuel. Gas-fired and electric barbecues being another since they do not require any special preparation of fuel.

Charcoal

Charcoal is generally available in two forms, as a lumpwood charcoal or as uniformly pressed briquets. Lumpwood charcoal is cheap and easy to light and gives off a good wood flavour; however, it does burn up rather faster than the compact briquets.

Charcoal in briquet form is highly recommended from the cook's point of view, since the briquets burn for a long time, with little smoke or odour, and produce a uniform intense heat.

Some brands of briquets are specially treated to ignite quickly; briquets without an ignition agent require several minutes of intense heat before they ignite. When burning they simply glow instead of flaming, unless there is a considerable amount of draught. In daylight you cannot usually see the glow, just a fine grey ash that appears on the surface of the briquet as the fire spreads through it.

Wood

Soft woods such as pine, cedar and birch are good for kindling a fire since they burn quickly. However, they do tend to flare and give off smoke, so hard woods, such as oak, ash and beech, should be added later to burn more slowly and give a hotter fire.

Aromatic woods can be added to the fire to give a delicious flavour and aroma to the food being cooked.

A wood fire is not made by simply building a random pile of wood. Sticks of kindling should be arranged over crumpled paper to form a 'wig-wam'. This shape allows air to get in and feed the fire. Once the sticks are burning, keep adding larger pieces of hard wood until you have a fire of the right size. Always wait until the last pieces are burning well before adding new. It will be ready for cooking in 20–30 minutes.

THE FIRE

Where to set up the grill

For safety's sake, the grill should be located away from trees, dry grass and bushes. And for your neighbours' sake, locate the grill where smoke won't be a bother. Check the direction of the wind and place the windscreen, if there is one, to shield the coals; but take advantage of any light prevailing wind which will help to get the fire started.

Barbecuing indoors is not recommended, as the carbon monoxide it produces is deadly. However, a small barbecue like a hibachi can be used in the fireplace with the draught open, providing there is good ventilation.

Building the fire

Line the fire-bowl of any charcoal-burning barbecue with heavy duty aluminium foil; shiny side out — this will aid cleaning up. The foil will also reflect heat back on to the food, speeding cooking time.

Spread a shallow layer of sand or gravel on the bottom before adding the briquets. This layer will catch any dripping fat, so reducing smoking and flare-ups. It will also protect the metal of the barbecue from intense heat and help to produce a good draught at lower levels. Gravel can be washed and used again providing it has been thoroughly dried.

If there is a draught control, open this before attempting to start the fire, as it will introduce air to the lower levels.

Lighting the fire

Never use petrol, lighter fluid, kerosene or a similar volatile fluid. Apart from their more obvious dangers they also leave a nasty taste in the food.

Self-igniting charcoal
Perhaps the simplest, though not the cheapest or quickest method of starting a fire is to buy a small pack of specially treated briquets. The pack is placed on the fire-bed and lit. The contents are in turn ignited and the coals should be ready in 30–40 minutes.

Fire lighters
The familiar solid white block fire starter has been available from hardware shops for many years and has always been popular as a cheap, safe and efficient domestic fire starter. Break off two or three pieces and place them between the base and halfway up the sides of the charcoal pyramid. After lighting, the starter will burn for 15 minutes. The coals should be ready for cooking in 20–30 minutes.

Skewered noisettes of lamb (see recipe page 53)

The same solid white starter is now available in granulated form. This provides a slightly faster ignition than the solid block. Build a pyramid of briquets and sprinkle the granules in the air spaces to allow a 'wicking' action. The granules can be safely lit with a match or taper at several points. This ensures a quick spread of fire and the coals should be ready for cooking in 20–30 minutes.

Liquid fire starter
Carefully follow the manufacturer's instructions. Arrange a pyramid of 20–25 briquets on the fire-bed or brazier, then pour liquid on to the cold briquets. Wait for the liquid to soak in, then light the briquets with a taper. The fire is ready for cooking when most of the briquets are covered in grey ash, 30–45 minutes.

Keeping a small supply of briquets that have been previously soaked in liquid fire starter will help to speed up this process.

Jellied alcohol or canned heat
Arrange a pyramid of briquets directly on the fire-bed. Place two or three teaspoons of the jelly well down into the cavities near the base of the pile. Close and remove the jelly container before lighting the jelly. The coals should be ready for cooking in 30–40 minutes.

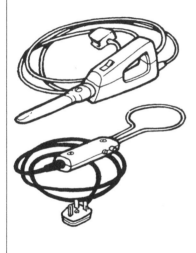

Electric fire starters
Portable electric fire starters provide a sure, fast and clean method of starting the fire. The electric starter element is placed near the base of the briquet pyramid and some 5–10 minutes after being switched on can be removed, as by then the briquets should be burning properly. Remake the pile, using long-handled tongs, and 20–30 minutes after starting the briquets should be ready for cooking. Some of the more expensive barbecues have a built-in electric fire starter.

Gas torch or blow lamp
Fast results can be achieved by using one of the compact pressure torches normally used for paint stripping etc. Arrange briquets one layer deep, but close together. Slowly pass the flame over the briquets until the fire is visibly started. The coals will be ready for cooking in 30–40 minutes.

Managing the fire

Once the fire has been properly lit and an adequate fire-bed prepared, the only problem that remains is that of heat control. A fire should be lit 15–45 minutes before it is needed for cooking.

Lemon and rosemary basted chicken (see recipe page 59)

Adding more charcoal

When cooking large roasts or for a large gathering you may need to add more coals during cooking. Keep some extra briquets at the edge of the grill so you have a reserve of hot coals. These can be moved into position with the burning coals and will ignite more quickly than unheated coals.

Controlling the heat

Heat should be even, so if the fire becomes too hot, simply raise the grill further up from the heat, or move hot briquets out to the side and bring in cooler ones. Old cinders from a previous barbecue placed on the coals will also effectively lower the heat.

For a hotter fire, move the grill and food closer to the fire, increase the draught or brush the grey ash from the top of the charcoal.

The draughts in your barbecue, if there are any, are there to control heat too. Opening them lets in more air, increasing the heat. Closing them lowers the heat.

Do not cook food over flames or thick smoke. Aim for a radiant fire, that will glow red by night but look grey during daylight.

Snuffing the fire

When your cooking session is finished, snuff out the coals and store them for later use. In covered barbecues the snuffing is done simply by closing the dampers on top and bottom. With smaller units the coals can either be transferred to a metal bucket with a lid which, when closed, will fulfil the same function, or dunked into a bowl of water and left afterwards to dry out.

Never pour water over the barbecue itself to put out the coals; the sudden shock may warp or damage the metal.

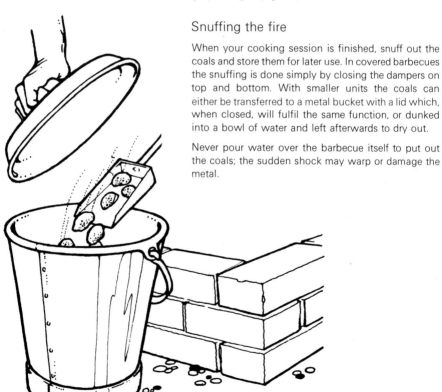

SAFETY

Everyone hopes their barbecue party will go by without any unfortunate incidents. However, it is always safe to have at hand an assortment of sprays, ointments, dressings and the like, just in case.

In an attempt to keep the party safe, remember not to hang lights or lanterns from trees, or on patio walls or steps where they could easily be pushed over. Keep paper lanterns away from lights and pin down any tablecloths if lights are nearby. In case of an emergency keep a fire-quelling bucket of sand or soil near to hand.

In case of accidents

Bug-repellent spray
Both the food and lights of your barbecue party will attract a host of insects. Lights set fairly high at a slight distance will keep the moths at bay, but for the others a spray may be the only answer. However, avoid spraying over open food.

Burn lotion
A jar of some effective lotion or ointment, or the old-fashioned remedy of linseed oil and lime-water, should form part of your standard barbecue burn kit.

First-aid kit
Apart from bugs and burns your party should be free of incident, but for safety's sake have plasters, antiseptic and standard ointments near at hand.

ACCESSORIES

Basically very little extra equipment is needed for barbecues, but some implements do make things easier and safer for those handling the fire. Any tools you do buy should be sturdy in design and able to stand up to a certain amount of rough treatment.

If you hold regular barbecues, the accessories are best stored all together in a large bag or box to save searching on every barbecue occasion. Some of the essentials are listed below.

For the fire

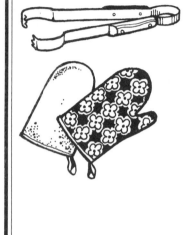

Tongs A long-handled pair of tongs with good gripping ends for arranging the fire and for turning food.

Oven gloves Asbestos gloves or mittens for those who handle the fire, plus oven gloves for lifting pots and pans from the grill.

Sprinkler bottle A large bottle with a sprinkler top, such as those used for dampening clothes, or a water pistol, to douse over-exuberant flames.

Bellows or fan Or even a rolled up newspaper to keep on hand for reviving a dying fire.

Work surface Working from the ground is difficult and dangerous, so try to erect a small table near the barbecue for preparation work. A household or garden trolley would suffice just as well, but heat-proof mats should be placed on the surface if made of wood or plastic.

For cooking

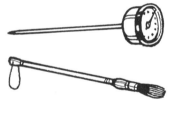

Meat thermometer A luxury unless you intend to spit roast or cook large roasts on the barbecue. Choose an all metal one which is unpainted.

Basting brush A small brush or tube-baster is useful for basting food with oil, butter or sauce.

Fork and spatula A long-handled fork and spatula for turning food safely.

Long skewers Long skewers for kebabs which may be made simply of metal or special steel. Choose ones with fire-proof handles or hand-guards for protection. If yours have decorative handles place these well away from the fire.

Cooking foil Invaluable for wrapping and covering food, useful for lining tins and drip trays. It can also be used, shiny side out, to line the fire-bowl, thus increasing its heat effectiveness. Keep a variety of widths and thicknesses for varying purposes.

Hinged wire grill Sometimes known as a flip-grill, this has long handles and is very useful for cooking

hamburgers, small chops, steak or fish because they can all be easily turned at once. If any fat should fall on the fire and flare up, the food can also be easily lifted from the grill until the flares have died down.

Pots and pans Long-handled pots and pans with heavy bases to keep sauces, etc. hot on the grill.

Fireproof pots Small ones which will be needed for bastes, marinades, oil or melted butter.

Knives Preparation of food for a barbecue needs at least the same array of sharp knives as you would use in the kitchen. If anything their quality should be higher, to overcome the hazards of working out of doors and on less than convenient work surfaces.

Spoons Again, long-handled and with a heat-resistant handle. Metal spoons become hot all too quickly and wooden ones are likely to get burned.

Boards Sturdy wooden boards for holding prepared foods and for cutting and carving those that are cooked.

Coffee pot Choose a strong metal coffee pot, leave it on the cool part of the grill and ask guests to help themselves. The coffee can be made indoors and then decanted into the pot to keep warm; alternatively you could use a coffee percolator and make the coffee from scratch on the barbecue.

Absorbent paper For mopping up and wiping hands.

Waste bin Adequate provision should be made, not only for the garbage you create during cooking but also to cope with paper napkins, plates and the like after use.

For serving

Salad and vegetable bowls Although it is customary for people to help themselves to the cooked food straight from the barbecue, you will need metal or wooden serving bowls for things like salads and vegetables; these are safer to handle than china, glass or plastic.

Cutlery Can be kept to a minimum, as much of what is traditionally cooked on the barbecue is finger food. Most plastic cutlery will do quite well and can be cleaned or thrown away as you like, but provide sharp knives for steaks.

Ice bucket As necessary as a good coffee pot, and for a similar reason; if the wine or punch is as hot as the food the party spirit will soon be lukewarm.

Can and bottle openers Essential, and to avoid losing them, tie with cord and attach to the serving table.

Pepper and salt A good large pepper mill and an equally sturdy salt-shaker are musts since a lot of people may want to re-season their food.

Paper napkins Large and strong for mopping up and for wiping sticky fingers as well as holding hot finger food.

Bread basket Lined with a paper or cloth napkin to keep any hot bread warm, it is the easiest way to cope with rolls, toast or sliced bread.

Plates, bowls and glasses Disposable items are usually much easier to handle and are less fragile as well as being easy to clear away. Choose between paper and plastic. If you do a lot of barbecuing, it may be worth investing in a set of melamine plates and dishes.

To clean

Metal brush To clean the grill and other metal parts to which food may stick. Do not wash as any coating left keeps the food from sticking next time the grill is used.

Oven cleaner To clean the fire-pan and the rest of the barbecue at the end of the season.

For thorough cleaning at the end of the season not only clean the fire-pan but also the spit-basket, forks, skewers, etc. in hot soapy water and dry well.

Store the equipment in a clean, dry place and cover with plastic to keep dry and clean during the winter months ahead.

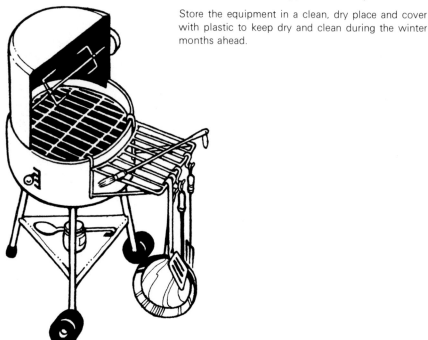

BARBECUE FAIRE

CHOICE OF FOOD

Many different foods including meat, poultry, fish and certain vegetables and fruit are suitable for cooking over charcoal. Some are ready to be barbecued as they are, with little or no preparation, whereas others may improve by being marinated first for several hours or basted during cooking. The general rule that it pays to buy the best quality applies especially to meat, which is probably one of the most popular foods cooked in this way. Try wrapping some foods in foil parcels, to seal in all the tasty juices. Pork chops (illustrated on page 114) can be particularly good done in this way.

Meat

Meat for barbecuing should be of the best quality you can afford and suitable for either roasting, grilling or frying. Meat-tenderisers, or the use of a good marinade, will enable you to barbecue less tender and cheaper cuts, such as flank, blade and chuck.

If using frozen meat, allow to thaw completely before cooking. The cut of meat and the way in which it is prepared will influence the amount you buy, but as a rough guide, allow 350–450 g/$\frac{3}{4}$–1 lb per person for meat with the bone in and 225 g/$\frac{1}{2}$ lb if the meat is boneless. Make sure the food is fairly even in size as it is then easier to estimate cooking times.

Poultry

For grill cooking, choose portions or joints; if you buy these rather than cutting up whole birds, you avoid having to use the back and any bony parts. Choose drumsticks, thighs, breast and wings, giving a good selection of light and dark meat.

Frozen poultry should be completely thawed before cooking. If using small birds, split down the back, remove the backbone and open flat for grilling. For spit-roasting, choose chicken or ducks weighing from 1–1·5 kg/2$\frac{1}{4}$–3$\frac{1}{2}$ lb; if barbecuing more than one, choose birds of a uniform weight. Boneless chicken, cut into pieces to put on skewers, makes excellent kebabs.

Fish

Whole fish, fish steaks or fillets and shellfish are all excellent barbecued, but as fish is more delicate and disintegrates over heat more quickly than meat, special care must be taken when cooking it. The grill must be well-oiled and hot, otherwise the fish will stick to it. A hinged grill (see page 24) makes it easier to turn fillets or small fish. Cubes of boneless fish may be threaded on skewers and marinated before cooking on an oiled grill.

Vegetables

Vegetables such as potatoes, corn and aubergines are suitable for cooking whole over the grill; others including tomatoes, onions, peppers and mushrooms are often threaded on skewers alternating with meat or fish in interesting combinations. Some vegetables which have an affinity for the smoky flavour of the barbecue may be cooked directly on the coals.

Fruit

Fruits do not need much cooking so they can usually be done after the main cooking is over, or if wrapped in foil they can be cooked at the edge of the fire at the same time.

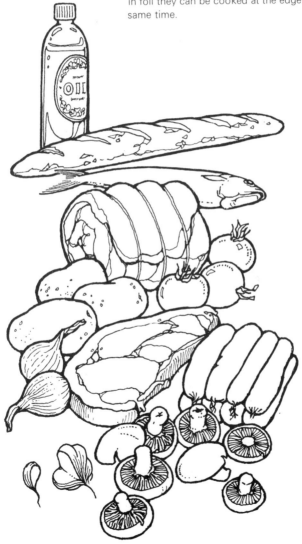

COOKING TIMES

Judging when food is cooked is an art that often comes only with experience. The food temperature, heat of the grill and other variables such as wind and humidity will all serve to alter cooking times.

The degree to which food is cooked will depend upon its thickness and its distance from the coals. So to achieve varying degrees of cooked meat it is necessary to alter the distance between the grill and fire, in order to have the food ready at the same time.

General advice on grilling and spit-roasting is given in the cooking tables, but after some experience your own judgement should serve as a reliable guide.

Grilling time chart

Food type	Cut	Size or weight	Fire heat	Approximate cooking time (each side) in minutes		
				Rare	Medium	Well done
Beef	steak	2·5 cm/ 1 inch	hot	5–6	7–8	10–12
	steak	3·5 cm/ 1½ inch	hot	6–7	9–10	12–15
	hamburger	2·5 cm/ 1 inch	medium	3–4	5–6	7–10
	skewer		hot	4–5	6–8	10–12
Lamb	chops	2·5 cm/ 1 inch	medium	5–6	7–8	10
	skewer		medium	5–6	7–8	10
Pork	chops	2–2·5 cm/ ¾–1 inch	medium			18–20
	sausages	individual	medium			8–10
	spareribs	whole	low/medium			1–1¼ hours
	skewer		medium			15–20
Poultry	chicken	split	medium			18–25
		portion	medium			15–20
	duck	split	medium			25
Veal	steaks or chops	2·5 cm/ 1 inch	medium			9–12
	skewer		medium			10–15
Fish	steak	1 cm/ ½ inch	medium			3–4
	steak	2·5 cm/ 1 inch	medium			5–7
	whole (small)	450–575 g/ 1–1¼ lb	medium			20
	whole (large)	1–1·25 kg/ 2–2½ lb	medium			45
	fillets	2 cm/ ¾ inch	medium			5–7
Lobster	split	450–675 g/ 1–1½ lb	medium/hot			14–15
Ham	steak	2·5 cm/ 1 inch	medium			10

Spit-roasting time chart

Food type	Cut	Size or weight	Fire heat	Rare	Medium	Well done
Beef				**60°C/140°F**	**70°C/160°F**	**90°C/190°F**
	rump (rolled)	1·5–2·25 kg/ 3–5 lb	medium	$1\frac{1}{2}$–2	$2\frac{1}{4}$–3	3–4
	sirloin	2·25–2·75 kg/ 5–6 lb	medium/hot	$1\frac{1}{4}$–$1\frac{3}{4}$	$2\frac{1}{4}$–3	3–4
	rolled rib	1·75–2·75 kg/ 4–6 lb	medium/hot	2–$2\frac{1}{2}$	$2\frac{1}{4}$–3	$3\frac{1}{4}$–$4\frac{1}{2}$
Lamb				**60°C/140°F**	**70°C/160°F**	**80°C/180°F**
	leg	1·5–3·5 kg/ $3\frac{1}{2}$–8 lb	medium	1–$1\frac{1}{4}$	$1\frac{1}{2}$–2	2–$3\frac{1}{4}$
	rolled shoulder	1·5–2·75 kg/ 3–6 lb	medium	1–$1\frac{1}{4}$	$1\frac{1}{2}$–2	2–$3\frac{1}{4}$
Pork						**85°C/185°F**
	shoulder	1·5–2·75 kg/ 3–6 lb	medium			2–3
	loin	1·5–2·25 kg/ 3–5 lb	medium			2–3
	spareribs	900 g–1·75 kg/ 2–4 lb	medium/hot			1–$1\frac{3}{4}$
	fresh ham	2·25–3·5 kg/ 5–8 lb	medium			$3\frac{1}{2}$–$4\frac{1}{2}$
Poultry						**90°C/190°F**
	chicken	1·25–2·25 kg/ $2\frac{1}{2}$–5 lb	medium			1–$1\frac{1}{2}$
	turkey	4·5–8·25 kg/ 10–18 lb	medium			2–4
	duckling	1·75–2·75 kg/ 4–6 lb	medium			1–2
Veal						**90°C/190°F**
	leg	2·25–3·5 kg/ 5–8 lb	medium			2–3
	rolled shoulder	1·5–2·25 kg/ 3–5 lb	medium			$1\frac{1}{2}$–$2\frac{1}{2}$
	loin	2·25–2·75 kg/ 5–6 lb	medium			$1\frac{1}{2}$–$2\frac{1}{4}$
Fish						**50–55°C/ 120–130°F**
	large, whole	2·25–4·5 kg/ 5–10 lb	low/medium			$1\frac{1}{2}$–3
	small, whole	675 g–1·75 kg/ $1\frac{1}{2}$–4 lb	low/medium			$1\frac{1}{4}$–2

Note The temperatures refer to the temperature which should be reached on a meat thermometer. Insert the thermometer into the centre of the joint before cooking.

COOKING PROCEDURES

Procedures for cooking are just as important as cooking times to ensure an evenly cooked product.

On the grill

Knock off the ash from the briquets before starting to grill food. Brush the grill with a little oil to prevent meat from sticking. Place meat on the grill and barbecue 5–7·5 cm/2–3 inches above the coals. This will sear the food, sealing in and preserving the juices. After searing raise the grill to about 10 cm/4 inches above the coals.

On the spit

Spit cooking is an excellent and popular way to cook ribs of beef, loin of pork, ham, leg of lamb, poultry and large fish. Most hooded barbecues and wagon grills incorporate rôtisserie equipment, while separate attachments are available even for very small units. For practical purposes, the spit should be powered by an electric or battery-operated motor.

A good steel spit will be at least 5 mm/$\frac{1}{4}$ inch square, and have two forks. Each fork should have two, and preferably four, sharp tines which will pierce and firmly hold the meat. It is important to ensure the meat is properly balanced on the spit. Badly balanced meat will rotate in fits and starts, resulting in uneven cooking and heavy wear on the motor. With practice, you should be able to pass the spit through the centre of foods which have a uniform shape, such as a rolled roast.

After skewering the meat on the spit, carry out a balance test. Hold the spit in the palms of your hands and check its tendency to roll. Slowly rotate the spit on your palms — there should be no tendency to roll quickly from any position if the balance is even. If it does roll, re-skewer it to improve the balance, and if necessary use balancing weights to correct the drag. Very fat meat will shift its balance during cooking and may have to be re-spitted or balanced with a weight.

To safeguard against spit forks working loose during cooking, tighten them with pliers.

Various barbecue accessories can be used in conjunction with the spit. Spit baskets, made from wire, are available in flat or cylindrical form — the flat basket is not deep enough to allow food to turn over, whilst the cylindrical basket allows the food to 'tumble'. A shish-kebab attachment is useful for cooking several kebabs at one go and a hot dog wheel will impale up to a dozen sausages.

In the coals

To save space and to cook more of a meal at one time, several foods can be cooked directly in the fire-pan, either in the coals or at the side. Potatoes, whole aubergines, onions, etc, securely wrapped in a double thickness of foil, will cook here in the same way and the same time as a rather hot oven.

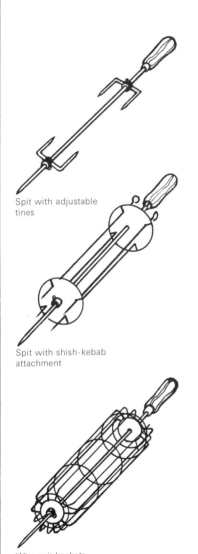

Spit with adjustable tines

Spit with shish-kebab attachment

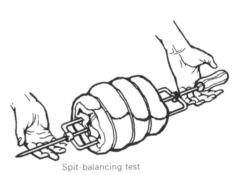

Spit-balancing test

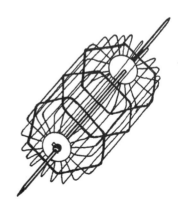

Wire spit baskets

COOKING AHEAD

Although a barbecue is meant to be an impromptu affair, if you are planning upon a large party it is wise to prepare some of the food beforehand, either complete or ready to reheat. Some food, like vegetable dishes or sauces, can be made in advance or cooked on the barbecue, depending on the grill space and time available.

Precooked food

Appetisers and desserts These are best prepared in advance and kept either in the refrigerator or freezer until required. The simplest dessert, ice cream, can be kept in the freezer right up to the last moment if it is of the soft scoop variety. Keep a stock of sweet sauces and whipped cream to go with it.

Salads These can be washed and prepared beforehand and kept chilled in the refrigerator until required.

Dressings Can be prepared well in advance and stored in a screw-topped jar. Before using, simply shake for 10 seconds to mix.

Meat Steak is spoilt by reheating but you can go a long way towards taking the load off your grill by pre-browning and pre-cooking items such as chicken portions, lamb and pork chops and sausages, then simply finishing the cooking and crisping on the barbecue itself.

Food from the freezer

Think of your freezer as a store-cupboard and you won't go far wrong. The weather hardly ever turns out to plan, so make sure you have a stock of steaks, chops, chicken portions, sausages, vegetables and bread ready for when the weather is kind.

Use it to store appetisers and desserts made well in advance of your barbecue party, as well as a stock of commercially prepared desserts such as cheesecakes, gâteaux and iced cakes.

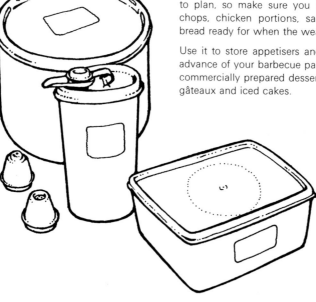

KEEPING FOOD HOT

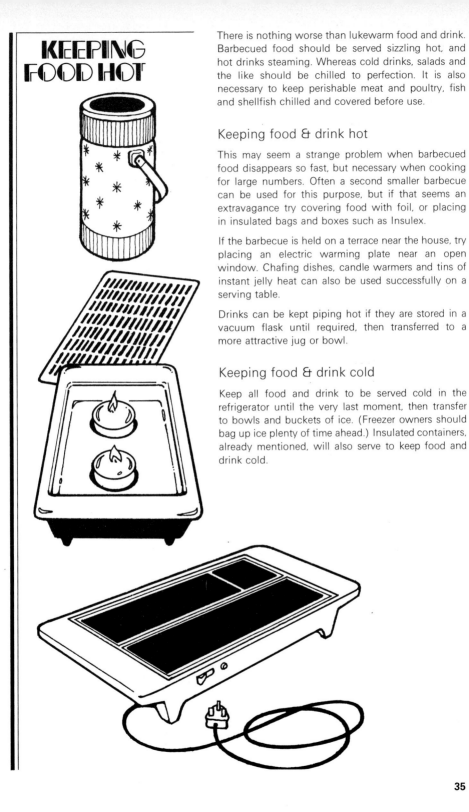

There is nothing worse than lukewarm food and drink. Barbecued food should be served sizzling hot, and hot drinks steaming. Whereas cold drinks, salads and the like should be chilled to perfection. It is also necessary to keep perishable meat and poultry, fish and shellfish chilled and covered before use.

Keeping food & drink hot

This may seem a strange problem when barbecued food disappears so fast, but necessary when cooking for large numbers. Often a second smaller barbecue can be used for this purpose, but if that seems an extravagance try covering food with foil, or placing in insulated bags and boxes such as Insulex.

If the barbecue is held on a terrace near the house, try placing an electric warming plate near an open window. Chafing dishes, candle warmers and tins of instant jelly heat can also be used successfully on a serving table.

Drinks can be kept piping hot if they are stored in a vacuum flask until required, then transferred to a more attractive jug or bowl.

Keeping food & drink cold

Keep all food and drink to be served cold in the refrigerator until the very last moment, then transfer to bowls and buckets of ice. (Freezer owners should bag up ice plenty of time ahead.) Insulated containers, already mentioned, will also serve to keep food and drink cold.

FLAVOURINGS

Flavourings are all important to a barbecue meal. Even though plain grilled meat, poultry, fish and shellfish are delicious in themselves, combined with a complementary flavouring they taste even better.

To satisfy all tastes, supply a large range of herbs, spices, sauces and dressings for guests to help themselves.

Herbs

Sprinkle on plain grilled meat, poultry, fish and shellfish, and on to coals to impart a delicious flavour and aroma to the same. Wherever possible try to use fresh herbs, but substitute good quality dried if this is not possible.

Add herbs to dressings and marinades as far ahead as possible, giving them plenty of time to fully flavour.

Bags of bouquet garni, secured on the end of a skewer, stick or fork, can be dipped in butter, oil or marinade; used as a basting brush will give food being cooked a delicate but recognisable herb flavour.

Spices and seasonings

Everyday spices and seasonings are excellent for flavouring barbecued food, but there are several specially prepared barbecue seasonings on the market which will give the right hot and spicy flavour to barbecued food.

Barbecued mackerel with dill (see recipe page 63), gooseberry herb sauce (see recipe page 94) and cucumber relish (see recipe page 103)

BARBECUE PARTIES

One of the prime advantages of moving a party outside the confines of the house is the opportunity it offers you to entertain a large number of people at one time — many more than you would be able to serve comfortably indoors. And this is where the barbecue party comes into its own. From informal to grand, the mood can be what you choose to make it.

Such a party calls for the same kind of planning that goes into any party — but on a bigger scale. Since you will have more guests, you will need more food, more help and probably more cooking equipment. One of the cheapest and most efficient ways of doing this is to pool equipment. Ask some of your guests to bring along their barbecues and then put them in charge of that grill. So while some are grilling meats or basting roasts, others can be tending to the vegetables, appetisers or desserts.

If you opt to do the complete party yourself, a buffet or help-yourself meal will be the easiest to manage. But whatever option you take, your party will still need careful planning.

Planning the menu

If at all possible suit the meal to the weather. On a cold day provide plenty of hot meats, spicy hot sauces, warm bread and steaming hot drinks. On a hot day, cool dishes like salads and fruit dishes will be very popular, with simple cooked meat or fish.

Choose the menu to suit the guests, too. If there are lots of children around provide plenty of finger food such as sausages, fish fingers and chicken drumsticks. For a smaller, informal gathering be more adventurous with steaks and fish and special desserts. For a large party, variety is the keyword.

Always try to serve food that is easy to handle, and keep to one main kind of meat or fish, unless it is a large gathering. Accompany with a salad and one or two vegetables, plenty of bread of different varieties, drinks and a dessert.

Quantities

An often quoted rule is to think of average indoor helpings and then to double them. Keep this in mind and you won't go far wrong. Appetites are large in the open air when the atmosphere is relaxed and food can be seen and smelt to be cooking.

Be just as generous with drinks. These will vary with the weather too; long cool drinks being popular on a hot day, warm coffee, mulled wine and spirit-based drinks being preferable on a cold.

Grilled steaks, mixed grill kebabs (see recipe page 51) and foil-wrapped jacket potatoes

Party pointers

Have plenty of everything — fire and food alike. Fresh air sharpens appetites. Leftovers can be used another day, but nothing will save a meal that is too little and too late.

Expect the unexpected. Have some plan worked out in case a sudden summer storm blows up. Move the guests to the porch or house. If your grill is portable, find a safe, well-ventilated place where you can move it. On a patio, a huge sun umbrella or makeshift canvas covering will protect the fire and the cook.

Make some arrangements for throwing a little light on the situation. Dusk quickly turns to dark.

Be prepared to cope with barbecue enemies — flies, ants and moths. There are many pest deterrents on the market.

Develop a definite plan for a clean-up. Scrape and stack plates in an orderly fashion, then carry them into the kitchen. You will want to spend what is left of the evening in a pleasant atmosphere.

Blue cheese dip

METRIC/IMPERIAL Makes 150 g/5 oz
100 g/4 oz Danish Blue cheese, softened
2 tablespoons single cream
6 large pecan nuts, finely crushed
1½ tablespoons finely chopped chives

Combine all the ingredients in a medium mixing bowl, beating with a wooden spoon until they are well blended. Serve at room temperature.

Spicy cheese and brandy dip

METRIC/IMPERIAL Makes 450 g/1 lb
275 g/10 oz Cheddar cheese, grated
75 g/3 oz butter
175 ml/6 fl oz single cream
½ teaspoon Tabasco sauce
4½ tablespoons brandy

Cream the cheese and butter together in a medium mixing bowl with a wooden spoon. Gradually beat in the cream, then the Tabasco sauce and brandy, beating until the mixture is smooth and thick. Serve at room temperature.

Crudités

METRIC/IMPERIAL
carrots
celery sticks
green and red peppers
cucumber
cauliflower
small tomatoes
spring onions
button mushrooms
chicory
radishes

Wash, trim and dry all of the vegetables. Cut the carrots, celery, green and red peppers and cucumber into thin strips. Separate the cauliflower into florets. Leave the tomatoes, spring onions and button mushrooms whole. Separate the chicory into leaves and cut the radishes into roses. Arrange on a large platter.

Serve with sea salt, ground black pepper and blue cheese dip or spicy cheese and brandy dip (see above).

Grilled grapefruit

Cooking time
15 minutes
Serves 6

METRIC/IMPERIAL
3 large grapefruit
3 tablespoons sherry (optional)
3 tablespoons honey or brown sugar
6 maraschino cherries

Cut each grapefruit in half, cutting loose the segments and removing pips. Place each half on a double thickness of aluminium foil and spoon about a half tablespoon of sherry and honey or brown sugar over it. Wrap the edges of the foil securely to enclose.

Cook on the grill, over medium coals, cut side up, for about 15 minutes. Remove, unwrap and top each grapefruit half with a maraschino cherry. Serve at once.

Gazpacho

Serves 4–6

METRIC/IMPERIAL
3 slices brown bread, cut into cubes
300 ml/$\frac{1}{2}$ pint canned tomato juice
2 cloves garlic, finely chopped
$\frac{1}{2}$ cucumber, peeled and finely chopped
1 green pepper, deseeded and chopped
1 red pepper, deseeded and chopped
1 medium onion, finely chopped
675 g/1$\frac{1}{2}$ lb tomatoes, peeled, deseeded and chopped
4$\frac{1}{2}$ tablespoons olive oil
2 tablespoons red wine vinegar
$\frac{1}{2}$ teaspoon salt
$\frac{1}{4}$ teaspoon black pepper
$\frac{1}{2}$ teaspoon marjoram

Place the bread cubes in a medium mixing bowl and pour over the tomato juice. Leave to soak for 5 minutes, then squeeze carefully to extract the excess juice. Transfer the soaked bread to a larger mixing bowl, reserving the juice.

Add the garlic, cucumber, peppers, onion and tomatoes to the bread and stir well to mix. Purée the ingredients together, either through a sieve or in the liquidiser. Stir in the reserved tomato juice. Add the oil, vinegar, salt, pepper and marjoram. Stir well to blend. Turn the soup into a deep tureen or serving dish and chill for at least 1 hour before serving.

Serve with bowls of chopped onion, peppers, cucumber and toasted bread croûtons.

Potted shrimps or prawns

Serves 4

50 g/2 oz butter
⅛ teaspoon ground mace
pinch of cayenne pepper
¼ teaspoon salt
¼ teaspoon black pepper
225 g/8 oz cooked shrimps or prawns
50 g/2 oz clarified butter, melted

In a large frying pan, melt the butter over moderate heat. When the foam subsides, stir in the mace, cayenne and seasoning. Add the shrimps or prawns and coat them thoroughly with the seasoned butter. Remove from the heat.

Spoon equal amounts of the mixture into four small pots, leaving a 5-mm/¼-inch headspace at the top. Pour 1 tablespoon of the clarified butter into each pot. Cover with foil and chill for 2 hours.

Remove from the refrigerator, discard foil and serve with brown bread and butter.

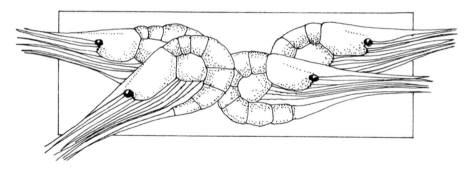

Kipper pâté

Cooking time
10–15 minutes
Serves 4

175 g/6 oz frozen buttered kipper fillets
40 g/1½ oz butter, softened
black pepper
grated nutmeg

Cook the kipper fillets as directed on the packet and turn the contents, including the juices, into a mixing bowl. Remove any skin and bone then mince or pound the kipper until quite smooth. Beat in the butter and season to taste with pepper and nutmeg. Turn into a small dish and chill before serving.

Serve with brown bread or crispbread.

Stilton pâté

Cooking time
20 minutes
Serves 8

METRIC/IMPERIAL
750 ml/1¼ pints milk
1 large onion, coarsely chopped
1 carrot, chopped
2 stalks celery, chopped
bouquet garni
75 g/3 oz butter
75 g/3 oz flour
3 tablespoons mayonnaise
2 teaspoons lemon juice
3 cloves garlic, crushed
10 stuffed olives, finely chopped
½ teaspoon salt
½ teaspoon black pepper
pinch of cayenne pepper
350 g/12 oz Stilton cheese, rind removed and crumbled

Pour the milk into a saucepan set over a high heat. Bring to the boil, reduce the heat and add the onion, carrot, celery and bouquet garni. Cover and simmer for 15 minutes. Remove from the heat and cool. Pour through a strainer into a large bowl, pressing the vegetables to extract any juice.

In a medium saucepan, melt the butter. Stir in the flour to make a smooth paste. Gradually add the milk, stirring constantly. Return to the heat and cook for 2–3 minutes, stirring, until the sauce is very thick and smooth. Set aside to cool to room temperature.

When the sauce is cool, beat in the mayonnaise, lemon juice, garlic and olives, and season with the salt, pepper and cayenne. Sieve the cheese into the mixture and beat until smooth.

Spoon into a serving dish and smooth the surface. Place in the refrigerator to chill for 1 hour before serving. Serve with hot buttered toast or rolls.

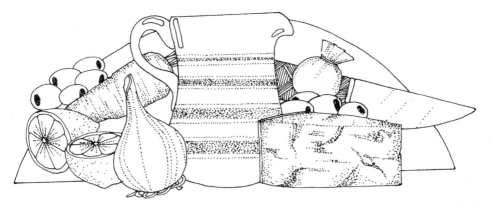

Melon boats

METRIC/IMPERIAL
2 small honeydew or ogen melons
2 pears, peeled, cored and chopped
100 g/4 oz black grapes, halved and pipped
2 teaspoons lemon juice
3 tablespoons clear honey
4 sprigs of mint

Cut the melons in half and remove the seeds. Using a small spoon or melon baller, scoop out the melon flesh in balls.

Transfer to a mixing bowl. Add the pears and grapes. Stir in the lemon juice and honey.

Scallop the edges of the melon halves with a sharp knife. Pile the fruit mixture back into the melon boats and chill for 20 minutes.

Just before serving, garnish each boat with a sprig of mint.

Mushrooms à la grecque

METRIC/IMPERIAL
25 g/1 oz onion, grated
2 tablespoons olive oil
200 ml/7 fl oz dry white wine
bouquet garni
1 clove garlic, peeled
salt and black pepper
350 g/12 oz button mushrooms
225 g/8 oz tomatoes, peeled
Garnish
chopped parsley

Cooking time
15 minutes
Serves 4

Sauté the onion in the oil until soft and transparent. Add the wine, bouquet garni and garlic. Season to taste with salt and black pepper.

Wipe the mushrooms clean but leave whole. Add to the onion mixture with the quartered and deseeded tomatoes. Cook gently, covered, for 5 minutes, then uncover for 5 more minutes to reduce the liquid by half. Remove from the heat and allow to cool. Remove the bouquet garni and garlic. Serve chilled in individual dishes sprinkled with chopped parsley.

MEAT, POULTRY AND GAME

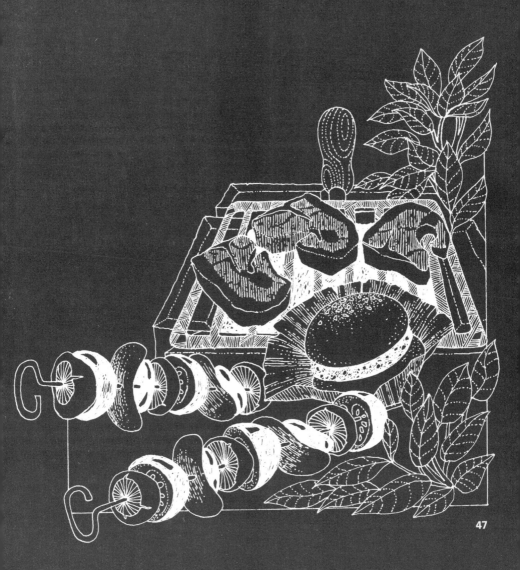

Steak au poivre flambé

METRIC/IMPERIAL
2 tablespoons black peppercorns
4 steaks, each about 2·5 cm/1 inch thick
2 large tomatoes
50 g/2 oz butter
pinch of dried oregano
pinch of garlic salt
4 tablespoons brandy

Cooking time
15–27 minutes
Serves 4

Illustrated on pages 66–67

Crush the peppercorns coarsely with a rolling pin and press into both sides of the steaks. Allow to stand at room temperature for about 30 minutes to absorb the flavour.

Barbecue, over hot coals, to the required degree: 6 minutes each side for rare meat, 8 minutes for medium meat and 10–12 minutes for well done meat. Transfer to a hot ovenproof serving dish.

Thickly slice the tomatoes and sauté in melted butter in a small pan over the barbecue until the slices are hot. Season with oregano and garlic salt to taste. Arrange the tomato slices on top of the steak. Warm the brandy, ignite and spoon, flaming, over the meat. Serve at once with barbecued vegetables, a salad and crusty French bread.

Cowboy steaks

METRIC/IMPERIAL
6 steaks, at least 2·5 cm/1 inch thick
300 ml/½ pint bacon drippings or cooking oil
4 tablespoons lemon juice
6 tablespoons finely chopped onion
1 tablespoon Worcestershire sauce
1 tablespoon horseradish sauce
½ teaspoon salt
⅛ teaspoon pepper
1 teaspoon paprika pepper
1 clove garlic, minced
2 bay leaves

Cooking time
14–30 minutes
Serves 6

Place the steaks in a single layer in a shallow pan. Melt the bacon drippings or heat the oil in a small saucepan, add the lemon juice, onion, Worcestershire sauce, horseradish, salt, pepper, paprika, garlic and bay leaves. Stir thoroughly and pour over the meat.

Allow the steaks to marinate for about 30 minutes, turning from time to time. Remove and barbecue over hot coals to the required degree: 7 minutes each side for rare meat, 9 minutes for medium meat and 12–15 minutes for well done meat. Baste with the marinade from time to time.

Basic hamburgers

Cooking time
6 minutes
Serves 6

METRIC/IMPERIAL
675 g/1½ lb good-quality minced beef
1 onion, finely minced
3 teaspoons salt
black pepper
6 soft bread rolls

Mix the beef and onion together, season well with the salt and pepper and shape into six hamburgers, each about 1 cm/½ inch thick. Barbecue over hot coals for 3 minutes on each side.

Serve in rolls, which should be toasted on the barbecue during the final few minutes of the hamburgers' cooking.

Variations
Cheddar cheese burgers Shortly after turning the burgers top each one with a slice of Cheddar cheese.
Cheese and bacon burgers Shortly after turning the burgers, sprinkle with grated cheese and start to grill 3 bacon rashers. When crisp the bacon rashers should be diced and scattered over the melting cheese.
Onion burgers (illustrated on page 95) Finely slice a medium onion and push into rings. Place in a small saucepan with a little melted butter and cook lightly until soft and golden. Shortly after turning the burgers, top each one with the onion rings.

Ginger teriyaki

Cooking time
6 minutes
Serves 6

METRIC/IMPERIAL
900 g/2 lb sirloin steak
Marinade
6 tablespoons soy sauce
1 tablespoon ground ginger
3 tablespoons sake or sherry
1 clove garlic, crushed
1 teaspoon sugar

Cut the steak into bite-sized pieces. Mix together the soy sauce, ginger, sake or sherry, garlic and sugar. Marinate the steak in this mixture for about 1 hour. Drain well.

Place the meat on six skewers and barbecue over hot coals for 6 minutes, turning from time to time. Baste with the remaining marinade during cooking.

Chilli beef chowder

METRIC/IMPERIAL
675 g/1½ lb braising steak
4 medium potatoes
225 g/8 oz carrots
2 onions
1 green pepper
1 clove garlic
salt and black pepper
1 tablespoon oil
2 teaspoons chilli powder
1 (227-g/8-oz) can tomatoes
1 (432-g/15¼-oz) can red kidney beans
1 tablespoon tomato puree
1·15 litres/2 pints beef stock
1 tablespoon flour

Cooking time
1¼ hours
Serves 6

Illustrated on page 56

Trim and discard any excess fat from the beef and cut into bite-sized cubes. Peel and dice the potatoes. Peel and finely dice the carrots and onions. Slice off 6 thin rings from the pepper and reserve. Cut the remainder into small dice, discarding seeds and pith. Peel and crush the garlic to a smooth paste with a little salt.

Heat the oil in a large, heavy-based pan and add the meat, vegetables and garlic. Fry for 3 minutes. Stir in the chilli powder and fry for 1 minute. Stir in the tomatoes, drained kidney beans, tomato purée, seasoning to taste, and stock. Bring to the boil, reduce heat, cover and simmer very gently for 45 minutes over low coals. Mix the flour with a little water to form a smooth paste. Stir into the chowder and continue cooking for a few more minutes, until thick.

Garnish the soup with the reserved pepper rings just before serving with wholemeal bread or rolls.

Orange-glazed pork loin

METRIC/IMPERIAL
1 (1·5–2·5-kg/3–5-lb) loin of pork
Sauce and glaze
40 g/1½ oz butter
100 g/4 oz brown sugar
1 (178-ml/6¼-fl oz) can frozen concentrated orange juice
4½ tablespoons water
2 teaspoons cornflour
100 g/4 oz green grapes, halved and pipped

Cooking time
1¼–2½ hours
Serves 6–8

Score the fat on the pork loin at 2·5-cm/1-inch intervals. Place the meat, fat side up, on the grill and cook over low coals, allowing 25–30 minutes per half kilo/per lb. Turn from time to time during cooking.

50

Meanwhile, heat the butter in a medium saucepan. Stir in the brown sugar. Add the concentrated orange juice and stir until smooth. Remove a little of this sauce to use as a baste for the pork. Stir the water into the cornflour and add gradually to the remaining orange sauce. Cook, stirring constantly, until the sauce thickens. Cook for a further 8 minutes. Add the grapes and serve with the pork.

Sweet 'n' sour spareribs

METRIC/IMPERIAL
1·75 kg/4 lb lean spareribs
1 teaspoon salt
Sauce
3 tablespoons soy sauce
3 tablespoons olive oil
150 ml/$\frac{1}{4}$ pint wine vinegar
150 g/5 oz brown sugar
6 tablespoons water
6 tablespoons pineapple juice
1 teaspoon grated root ginger or **$\frac{1}{4}$ teaspoon ground ginger**

Cooking time
1 hour 20 minutes
Serves 6–8

Rub the spareribs thoroughly with the salt. Place them directly on to the grill, over medium coals, and cook for 40 minutes, turning every 10 minutes.

Meanwhile, combine the remaining ingredients to make the sweet and sour sauce. After cooking for 40 minutes start brushing the spareribs with this and cook for a further 40 minutes until done — the meat will pull away easily from the end of the bone. Basting and turning should be a continuous process to ensure even flavouring and to prevent the ribs from becoming charred. Serve with honeyed pineapple (see page 114) and extra sweet and sour sauce.

Mixed grill kebabs

METRIC/IMPERIAL
8 lamb's kidneys
8 mushrooms
4 small tomatoes
8 small pork sausages
olive oil
salt and black pepper

Cooking time
15–20 minutes
Serves 4

Illustrated on page 38

Skin and halve the kidneys, removing cores. Wipe the mushrooms. Halve the tomatoes.

Thread the sausages, kidneys, mushrooms and tomatoes alternately on skewers. Brush with oil, season well and cook over low coals for about 15–20 minutes. Turn from time to time. Serve with a green salad and jacket potatoes.

Spicy lamb kebabs

METRIC/IMPERIAL
675 g/1½ lb boneless leg of lamb, cubed
12 shallots or small onions, peeled
12 button mushrooms
2 green peppers
Marinade
150 ml/¼ pint Worcestershire sauce
4 tablespoons water
2 tablespoons oil
1 onion, finely chopped
2 teaspoons sugar
1 teaspoon salt

Cooking time
30 minutes
Serves 6

Combine all the marinade ingredients in a saucepan, bring to the boil, cover and simmer for 10 minutes. Place the meat cubes in a bowl and pour over the marinade. Leave at room temperature for at least 2 hours.

Parboil the shallots until almost tender. Wipe the mushrooms clean, deseed the peppers and cut each into 12 pieces.

Arrange the lamb on the skewers alternately with the vegetables. Brush with the marinade and cook on an oiled grill, over hot coals, for 15 minutes, until brown on all sides. Baste continually with any remaining marinade.

Serve with cooked rice and tomato sauce (see page 93).

Skewered lamb meatballs

METRIC/IMPERIAL
100 g/4 oz sultanas
675 g/1½ lb boned shoulder of lamb
225 g/8 oz fresh white breadcrumbs
2 eggs, beaten
salt and black pepper
1 tablespoon curry powder
2 onions, sliced into rings

Cooking time
15–20 minutes
Serves 6

Illustrated on page 78

Soak the sultanas in water for 1 hour. Drain. Mince the lamb and mix with the breadcrumbs, sultanas, beaten eggs, seasoning and curry powder. Mix well together then shape into 12 meatballs. Arrange on to six skewers alternately with the onion rings. Grill, over hot coals, for 15–20 minutes, turning. Serve on a bed of outdoor pilaf (see page 79).

Note: Traditionally, these meatballs are enclosed in a caul before grilling, which your butcher may be able to supply, but this is optional.

Skewered noisettes of lamb

METRIC/IMPERIAL
4 noisettes of lamb
2 teaspoons made mustard
1 clove garlic, chopped
few sprigs of rosemary, crushed
8 shallots or small onions
8 small tomatoes
olive oil
salt and black pepper

Illustrated on page 19

Trim the noisettes of lamb and spread the mustard lightly on each side. Sprinkle with a little chopped garlic and crushed rosemary.

Peel and parboil the onions until almost tender. Thread on to skewers with the lamb noisettes and tomatoes. Brush with oil and season with salt and pepper. Grill over medium coals for 30 minutes, turning from time to time.

Serve with boiled rice and special barbecue sauce (see page 92).

Minted leg of lamb

METRIC/IMPERIAL
1 (1·75 kg–2·25-kg/4–5-lb) leg of lamb, boned and rolled
mint leaves
Marinade
50 g/2 oz brown sugar
3 tablespoons salad oil
1 teaspoon grated lemon rind
3 tablespoons lemon juice
3 tablespoons vinegar
4 tablespoons chopped mint leaves
1 teaspoon chopped tarragon leaves
1 teaspoon salt
1 teaspoon dry mustard

Mix together the ingredients for the marinade. Heat to boiling, reduce heat and simmer for 5 minutes. Cool. Place the lamb in a plastic bag or shallow dish. Pour the cooled marinade over the meat and leave to marinate for 24 hours.

Cook over medium coals, allowing 20–25 minutes per half kilo/per lb. During cooking baste with the marinade and throw fresh mint leaves on to the coals to give the lamb a delicious flavour and aroma.

Veal chops with Roquefort and mushroom stuffing

METRIC/IMPERIAL
4 veal chops
1 tablespoon olive oil
Stuffing
75 g/3 oz bacon rashers
100 g/4 oz button mushrooms
1 medium onion
50 g/2 oz Roquefort cheese, crumbled
50 g/2 oz parsley, chopped
salt and black pepper

Cooking time
35–40 minutes
Serves 4

Illustrated opposite

Cut the bacon into small dice and place in a saucepan. Heat gently until the fat runs, then add the cleaned and sliced mushrooms, chopped onion and a little oil if the mixture seems too dry. Cook for 2–3 minutes. Remove from the heat, allow to cool slightly then mix in the cheese, parsley and seasoning to taste.

Make a slit in each chop and place in the stuffing. Brush on both sides with the oil then secure each slit with wooden toothpicks or cocktail sticks. Place on the grill and cook over medium coals for 30 minutes, turning once. Remove cocktail sticks before serving with a crisp salad and crusty bread.

Note: If unable to obtain Roquefort, substitute Stilton or another good blue cheese.

Veal chops with Kirsch

METRIC/IMPERIAL
4 veal chops
1 tablespoon olive oil
salt and black pepper
3 tablespoons Kirsch
juice of 1 orange
chopped parsley

Cooking time
18–24 minutes
Serves 4

Brush the chops with the oil and season well on both sides. Grill over medium coals for 9–12 minutes on each side, until cooked. Place on a warmed serving dish.

Warm the Kirsch and pour over the veal chops. Ignite. When the flames die down add the orange juice and a little chopped parsley.

Veal chops with Roquefort and mushroom stuffing (see recipe above)

Bacon-wrapped sausages

METRIC/IMPERIAL
450 g/1 lb pork sausages
100 g/4 oz Cheddar cheese, sliced
8 rashers bacon
4 teaspoons made mustard

Cooking time
20 minutes
Serves 4

Illustrated on page 95

Barbecue the sausages over medium coals for about 15 minutes, then slit them lengthways, almost through. Fill with the cheese slices and press the sausages together again.

Spread the bacon rashers with mustard and wrap around the sausages, securing the ends with wooden cocktail sticks. Place on the grill again and cook over medium coals for a further 5 minutes, or until the cheese melts and the bacon is crisp. Serve with a mixed green salad and potato crisps.

Basic hot dogs

METRIC/IMPERIAL
6 frankfurters
6 long bread rolls
butter

Cooking time
6–10 minutes
Serves 6

Illustrated opposite

Place the frankfurters on the grill and cook for 6–10 minutes over medium coals, turning frequently. During the last few minutes of cooking, toast the bread rolls if liked. Remove from the heat and spread with butter. Fill with the frankfurters and serve with mustard, onions or tomato sauce.

Variations
Frankfurter and pineapple Slit open each frankfurter along its length and place a halved pineapple ring in the opening. Wrap a rasher of streaky bacon around the frankfurter and secure with wooden cocktail sticks. Grill until the bacon is crisp on all sides, about 8 minutes. Remove sticks before serving.
Cheese dogs Slit open each frankfurter along its length and lay in a long wedge-shaped piece of cheese. Cook, with the cheese uppermost, until the frankfurter is hot and the cheese has melted, about 8 minutes.

Basic hot dogs (see recipe above) and chilli beef chowder (see recipe page 50)

Spicy ham steaks

METRIC/IMPERIAL
4 ham or gammon steaks, 2·5-cm/1-inch thick
honeyed pineapple (see page 112)
Marinade
150 ml/¼ pint sherry
150 ml/¼ pint pineapple juice
2 tablespoons salad oil
pinch of ground cloves
1 tablespoon dry mustard
4 tablespoons brown sugar
1 teaspoon paprika pepper

Cooking time
20 minutes
Serves 4

Snip along the edges of the ham steaks to prevent them curling up. Mix all the ingredients for the marinade together. Marinate the ham for 2–3 hours, turning occasionally.

Remove the ham from the marinade and grill over low to medium coals for about 20 minutes, basting with the remaining marinade from time to time.

Serve hot with the honeyed pineapple.

Devilled chicken

METRIC/IMPERIAL
4 large chicken portions
2 teaspoons salt
2 teaspoons sugar
1 teaspoon pepper
1 teapoon ground ginger
1 teaspoon dry mustard
½ teaspoon curry powder
50 g/2 oz butter
Baste
2 tablespoons tomato ketchup
1 tablespoon mushroom ketchup
1 tablespoon Worcestershire sauce
1 tablespoon soy sauce
1 tablespoon plum jam
dash of Tabasco sauce

Cooking time
30 minutes
Serves 4

Place the chicken portions in a large shallow dish. Mix together the salt, sugar, pepper, ginger, mustard and curry powder and rub into the chicken. Leave for 1 hour.

Melt the butter and brush over the chicken. Grill for 20 minutes, over medium coals, until crisp, turning.

Mix the remaining ingredients together and any remaining butter. Heat gently and use to baste the chicken. Cook for a further 10 minutes, basting with this sauce from time to time. Heat any remaining sauce and serve with the chicken.

Lemon and rosemary basted chicken

METRIC/IMPERIAL
4 chicken portions
Baste
75 g/3 oz butter
2 tablespoons lemon juice
1 teaspoon salt
$\frac{1}{4}$ teaspoon white pepper
$\frac{1}{2}$ teaspoon paprika pepper
sprigs of rosemary

Cooking time
40 minutes
Serves 4

Illustrated on page 20

Wash the chicken portions and pat dry with absorbent paper. Melt the butter and combine with the remaining ingredients.

Place the chicken portions on the grill and barbecue over medium coals, brushing occasionally with the basting sauce during cooking. Turn every few minutes to ensure the chicken is well browned and evenly cooked. Cook for 40 minutes. Just before the end of cooking, throw a few more sprigs of rosemary on the coals to impart a delicious flavour to the chicken.

Serve with grilled tomatoes and orange and lemon barbecue sauce (see page 92).

Barbecued chicken drumsticks

METRIC/IMPERIAL
8 chicken drumsticks
Baste
50 g/2 oz butter
1 onion, grated
1 (227-g/8-oz) can tomatoes
2 tablespoons Worcestershire sauce
25 g/1 oz demerara sugar
1 teaspoon salt
black pepper

Cooking time
50 minutes
Serves 4

Trim away any excess skin from the drumsticks. Combine all the baste ingredients in a small saucepan, cover and simmer for 30 minutes. Rub through a sieve or liquidise until smooth.

Brush the drumsticks with the glaze and cook, over medium coals, for 10 minutes. Turn and cook for a further 10 minutes. Brush with the baste several times during cooking. Heat any remaining baste and serve with the chicken drumsticks.

Chinese duckling

METRIC/IMPERIAL
1 duckling
2 egg yolks
2 tablespoons soy sauce
3 tablespoons honey

Cooking time
45–60 minutes
Serves 2–4

Depending upon the size of the duckling, split in half or divide into quarters. Rub with a mixture of the egg yolks, soy sauce and honey.

Grill, cut side down, for 45–60 minutes, over medium to low coals, turning from time to time. Towards the end of the cooking time raise the heat to crisp the skin.

Skewered rabbit with mustard

METRIC/IMPERIAL
450 g/1 lb boneless rabbit meat
salt and pepper
4 teaspoons made mustard
4 teaspoons olive oil

Cooking time
15 minutes
Serves 4

Illustrated on page 96

Trim and cut the rabbit meat into serving-size pieces. Thread on to skewers and season with salt and pepper. Brush lightly with the mustard and then with the oil.

Barbecue, over medium to hot coals, for 15 minutes, turning from time to time. Serve with additional mustard sauce (see page 97) and jacket potatoes.

Note: For those guests who do not like mustard substitute redcurrant jelly for this.

FISH AND SHELLFISH

Grilled sardines

METRIC/IMPERIAL
12 fresh sardines
2 tablespoons oil
salt and black pepper
herb butter (see page 106)

Cooking time
10 minutes
Serves 4

Illustrated on page 113

Clean the fish and brush them with the oil. Season to taste with the salt and pepper and grill, over hot coals, for 10 minutes, turning once.

Remove from the heat and serve with pats of herb butter and a dish of ratatouille (see page 80).

Grilled trout

METRIC/IMPERIAL
4 trout, weighing 350 g/12 oz each
Marinade
3 tablespoons olive oil
1 medium onion, finely chopped
1 teaspoon French mustard
1 tablespoon chopped chives
2 tablespoons chopped dill
1 teaspoon salt
1 tablespoon lemon juice
½ teaspoon black pepper
2 tablespoons melted butter
herb butter (see page 106)

Cooking time
12 minutes
Serves 4

Clean and bone the trout and, if desired, remove the heads. Flatten out the fish and place them flesh side down in a shallow dish.

Prepare the marinade by combining the oil, onion, mustard, chives, dill, salt, lemon juice and pepper. Mix thoroughly. Pour the marinade over the fish and put in the refrigerator for 1 hour, turning once.

Place the fish, flesh side down, on an oiled grill and cook, over medium to hot coals, for about 4 minutes. Turn the fish over, brush with the melted butter and continue grilling for another 8 minutes, or until the skin of the trout is crisp and the flesh is easily flaked.

Remove from grill and serve with herb butter.

Baked stuffed fish

METRIC/IMPERIAL
1 whole cod, haddock or salmon, weighing 1·25–1·5 kg/2½–3 lb
Stuffing
1 onion, chopped
2 sticks celery, chopped
3 rashers bacon, chopped and fried until crisp
2 tablespoons chopped parsley
40 g/1½ oz fresh white breadcrumbs
50 g/2 oz butter, melted
salt and black pepper

Cooking time
$1-1\frac{1}{4}$ hours
Serves 4–6

Clean and gut the fish, removing the head if desired. Mix the stuffing ingredients together and place in the cavity of the fish, closing the opening with wooden cocktail sticks. Place on a large piece of buttered foil, season well, then wrap up securely.

Cook over medium coals for $1-1\frac{1}{4}$ hours, or until the fish flakes easily with a fork. Turn from time to time during cooking.

Barbecued mackerel with dill

METRIC/IMPERIAL
4 medium mackerel
2 tablespoons salad oil
juice of 1 lemon
salt and black pepper
sprigs of dill
gooseberry herb sauce (see page 94)
cucumber relish (see page 103)

Cooking time
20 minutes
Serves 4

Illustrated on page 37

Clean the mackerel, removing the heads if desired. Slash the flesh diagonally on each side of the fish about three times. Brush with the oil and lemon juice. Season to taste and scatter with the sprigs of dill.

Grill over medium coals for 10 minutes on each side, turning once and brushing from time to time with the oil and lemon juice. Serve with gooseberry herb sauce and cucumber relish.

Skewered plaice

METRIC/IMPERIAL
12 rashers streaky bacon
450 g/1 lb plaice fillets
150 ml/¼ pint seafare marinade (see page 100)
seafood sauce (see page 98)

Cooking time
10 minutes
Serves 4

Illustrated opposite

Place the bacon rashers on a board and stretch with the back of a round-bladed knife. Cut each rasher in half. Remove the skin from the plaice fillets and divide into 24 pieces. Place each on a halved rasher of bacon and roll up. Secure with a wooden cocktail stick. Place in a dish with the seafare marinade and leave to marinate for 2 hours.

Remove from the marinade, remove cocktail sticks and place on four skewers. Grill on the barbecue, over medium coals, for 8–10 minutes, turning and brushing from time to time with the marinade. Serve hot with seafood sauce and crusty bread.

Marinated salmon steaks with capers

METRIC/IMPERIAL
6 individual salmon steaks
Marinade
6 tablespoons capers
4 tablespoons olive oil
juice of 1 lemon
1 small onion, grated
3 shallots, finely chopped
salt and black pepper
thyme
bay leaves

Cooking time
20 minutes
Serves 6.

Mix the ingredients for the marinade together, beating to combine. Place in a shallow dish with the salmon steaks and leave to marinate for 2 hours.

Drain the salmon and grill, over medium coals, for 15–20 minutes, basting with the marinade and turning from time to time. Serve hot with any remaining marinade.

Opposite: Skewered plaice (see recipe above)
Overleaf: Corn on the grill (see recipe page 75), jacket potatoes (see recipe page 74), foil-wrapped onions (see recipe page 74) and steak au poivre flambé (see recipe page 48)

Tuna steaks with mustard

Cooking time
20 minutes
Serves 4

METRIC/IMPERIAL
50 g/2 oz butter, melted
3 teaspoons made mustard
1 tablespoon lemon juice
salt and black pepper
4 individual tuna or cod steaks
Garnish
lemon slices

Illustrated opposite

Combine the melted butter with the mustard, lemon juice and seasoning to taste. Brush half this mixture over the steaks, on both sides, then grill over medium coals for 10 minutes. Turn, brush with the remaining mixture and grill for a further 10 minutes.

Serve hot, with any of the remaining mustard mixture and lemon slices to garnish. Ratatouille (see page 80) would go well with this.

Orange grilled fish

Cooking time
15 minutes
Serves 6

METRIC/IMPERIAL
900 g/2 lb firm white fish
Marinade
4 tablespoons soy sauce
2 tablespoons tomato ketchup
2 tablespoons chopped parsley
150 ml/$\frac{1}{4}$ pint orange juice
grated rind of $\frac{1}{2}$ orange
salt and black pepper

Cut the fish into 2·5-cm/1-inch pieces. Mix the ingredients for the marinade together, beating well. Pour over the fish and leave to marinate for 1 hour.

Drain the fish and thread on six skewers. Grill over hot coals for about 8 minutes, then turn and grill for a further 7 minutes. Baste with the marinade during cooking.

Tuna steaks with mustard (see recipe above)

Grilled fish steaks

METRIC/IMPERIAL
6 individual fish steaks (cod, haddock or halibut)
1 teaspoon salt
¼ teaspoon pepper
50 g/2 oz butter, melted
1 tablespoon lemon juice
1 teaspoon chopped parsley or chives

Cooking time
10–15 minutes
Serves 6

Sprinkle the fish with the salt and pepper. Mix together the melted butter, lemon juice and parsley or chives. Brush the fish with this mixture. Place the fish steaks on a greased hinged grill and barbecue, over medium coals, for 10–15 minutes, turning once. Baste with the remaining lemon butter towards the end of the cooking time.

Seafood kebabs

METRIC/IMPERIAL
6 rashers streaky bacon, rinds removed
225 g/8 oz plaice fillets
salt and black pepper
3 crayfish tails, peeled
8 large cooked prawns, peeled
1 large lemon, cut into 4 thick slices
seafood sauce (see page 98)
Marinade
1 lemon
150 ml/¼ pint olive oil
1 clove garlic, crushed
¼ teaspoon salt
black pepper
1 bay leaf

Cooking time
10 minutes
Serves 4

Prepare the marinade first by carefully paring the rind from the lemon. Add the rind to the juice squeezed from the lemon, the oil, garlic, salt, pepper and bay leaf. Mix together thoroughly.

Place the bacon rashers on a board and stretch with the back of a round-bladed knife. Cut each rasher into two. Remove the skin from the plaice fillets and divide the fish into twelve pieces. Place each piece on a rasher of bacon, season and roll up, enclosing the fish. Secure each with a wooden cocktail stick. Cut each crayfish tail into four pieces. Place the bacon rolls, prawns and crayfish in the marinade and leave for 2 hours, turning occasionally.

Remove from the marinade. Cut each lemon slice into four pieces. Remove the cocktail sticks from the bacon rolls and put them with the prawns and crayfish on four long or eight short skewers, alternating with the pieces of lemon.

Place the skewers on an oiled grill and cook over medium coals for about 10 minutes, turning and brushing occasionally with the marinade. Serve with seafood sauce.

Mussel and bacon kebabs

METRIC/IMPERIAL
2·25 litres/4 pints fresh mussels
1 egg, beaten
fine white breadcrumbs
225 g/8 oz streaky bacon, rinds removed
cooking oil
salt and black pepper
lemon wedges

Cooking time
3–5 minutes
Serves 6

Clean the mussels and put them into a large pan with 300 ml/½ pint water. Heat until the shells open. Remove the mussels from their shells, dip in beaten egg and toss in breadcrumbs.

Flatten the bacon rashers with the back of a round-bladed knife until they are very thin. Cut each rasher in half and roll. Place the mussels and bacon rolls alternately on skewers. Brush with the oil and season generously. Cook over hot coals for 3–5 minutes, turning frequently. Serve with lemon wedges and a tartare sauce, if liked.

Spicy skewered shrimps

METRIC/IMPERIAL
450 g/1 lb large shrimps, shelled
lemon slices
Marinade
1 teaspoon chilli powder
1 tablespoon vinegar
1 clove garlic, crushed
salt and black pepper
1 teaspoon chopped parsley
6 tablespoons salad oil

Cooking time
6–10 minutes
Serves 4

Mix the marinade ingredients together, beating to combine well. Marinate the shrimps in this mixture for 2 hours. Remove from the marinade and thread on to four skewers.

Grill over medium coals for 6–10 minutes, turning occasionally and basting with the marinade. Serve hot with slices of lemon.

Grilled stuffed crab

METRIC/IMPERIAL

450 g/1 lb crab meat
4 tablespoons melted butter
25 g/1 oz parsley, finely chopped
2 tablespoons lemon juice
¼ teaspoon salt
pinch of cayenne pepper
6 cleaned and buttered crab shells
Garnish
lemon wedges
sprigs of watercress

Cooking time
15 minutes
Serves 6

Combine and blend in the liquidiser the crab meat, butter, parsley, lemon juice, salt and cayenne. Divide the mixture into six equal portions and stuff the prepared shells. Wrap each crab shell in two sheets of heavy duty aluminium foil. Place on the grill and barbecue, over hot coals, for about 15 minutes or until the shells turn brown.

Remove from grill and garnish with lemon wedges and watercress sprigs. Serve with brown bread and butter.

Barbecued lobster

METRIC/IMPERIAL

2 (675-g/1½-lb) lobsters
melted butter
lemon juice
salt and black pepper

Cooking time
20 minutes
Serves 4

To kill a live lobster drive the point of a sharp knife right through the natural cross on the head under which the brain lies, then split in half down the back. Remove the bag in the head and the intestine, a thin grey or black line running down through the tail meat. Crack the large claws with a hammer.

Put the prepared lobster halves on the grill, shell side down, brush with butter and barbecue over hot coals for 15 minutes, basting from time to time with the butter, lemon juice and seasoning. Turn and barbecue for 5 minutes longer. Serve with melted butter and lemon juice.

VEGETABLES

Jacket potatoes

METRIC/IMPERIAL
4 large potatoes
butter

Cooking time
50 minutes
Serves 4
Illustrated on pages 66–67

Scrub the potatoes and dry. Rub with a little butter and wrap in heavy duty aluminium foil. Place in the centre of the grill and cook, over medium coals, for about 50 minutes. Potatoes will be cooked when soft.

To serve, open the foil and cut a cross in the top of each potato. Fill with butter, soured cream and chives, cottage cheese or crumbled cooked bacon.

Sizzled potato chips

METRIC/IMPERIAL
450 g/1 lb fresh or frozen potato chips
1 onion, finely chopped
salt and black pepper
50 g/2 oz butter

Cooking time
25–40 minutes
Serves 4

Divide the chips into four equal portions and place each on a square of aluminium foil. Sprinkle with the chopped onion and seasoning to taste and dot with the butter. Fold the foil in to secure packages and cook, over medium coals, 40 minutes for fresh potato chips or 25 minutes for frozen, turning from time to time.

Foil-wrapped onions

METRIC/IMPERIAL
4 large onions
25 g/1 oz butter, melted
2 teaspoons Worcestershire sauce
salt and black pepper

Cooking time
45–60 minutes
Serves 4

Illustrated on pages 66–67

Peel and wash the onions and place each one on a square piece of foil. Brush with the melted butter and Worcestershire sauce and season to taste. Wrap the foil halfway up the sides of the onion and cook over medium coals for 45–60 minutes, turning every 10 minutes.

The onions are cooked when they feel soft to the touch. Remove the foil and any blackened skin before serving.

Corn on the grill

METRIC/IMPERIAL
4 fresh corn on the cobs (husks intact)
salt and black pepper
Golden glow butter
100 g/4 oz butter
2 tablespoons sieved pimiento
½ teaspoon onion powder (optional)
½ teaspoon paprika pepper

Cooking time
30 minutes
Serves 4

Illustrated on pages 66–67

Remove the large outer husks from the corn, turn back the inner husks and remove silks. Set aside.

Prepare golden glow butter by mixing together the remaining ingredients with a wooden spoon until thoroughly combined. Spread each corn with the softened butter. Pull the husks back over the ears and roast on the grill, over medium to hot coals, for 30 minutes, turning frequently.

Serve hot, with any remaining butter and seasoning to taste.

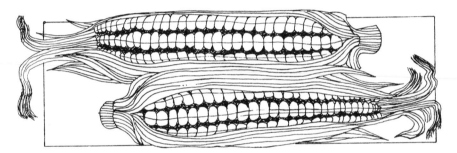

Stuffed grilled mushrooms

Cooking time
20 minutes
Serves 4

METRIC/IMPERIAL
24 large open cap mushrooms
salad oil
2 cloves garlic (optional)
1 medium onion
4 tablespoons chopped parsley
salt and black pepper

Remove the stalks from the mushrooms and set aside. Wipe the caps clean then brush with salad oil and grill, over medium to low coals, for about 15 minutes.

Meanwhile, chop the garlic and onion until fine and mix with the parsley and seasoning to taste. When the mushrooms are almost cooked, put a spoonful of the mixture in the centre of each mushroom cap and cook for a further 5 minutes.

Grilled red peppers

METRIC/IMPERIAL
4 large red peppers
1 medium onion
6 tablespoons French dressing (see page 88)

Cooking time
5–10 minutes
Serves 4
Illustrated opposite

Cook the peppers over a hot grill until the skins begin to blacken. Remove from the grill and peel off the skins. Slice into quarters, removing all seeds and pith. Peel and finely chop the onion. Mix the peppers and onion together and place in a small dish. Pour the French dressing over the still warm peppers and marinate for 30 minutes before serving with barbecued beef, chops or sausages.

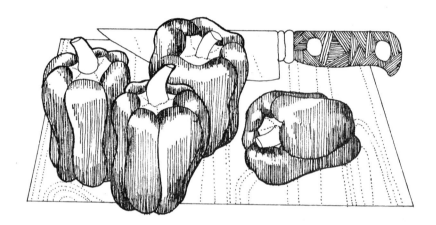

Cheesy-topped tomatoes

METRIC/IMPERIAL
8 medium tomatoes
salad oil
1 medium onion
4 tablespoons finely chopped parsley
75 g/3 oz fresh white breadcrumbs
salt and black pepper
16 small slices cheese

Cooking time
10 minutes
Serves 4

Cut the tomatoes in half and scoop out the seeds. Brush the insides with salad oil. Chop the onion finely and add to the parsley and breadcrumbs. Mix well, season to taste and use to stuff the hollow tomatoes.

Grill, over low coals, for about 5 minutes. Top each half tomato with a slice of cheese and cook for a further 5 minutes. Serve with lamb chops, burgers or sausages.

Grilled red peppers (see recipe above)

Outdoor pilaf

Cooking time
30 minutes
Serves 4

METRIC/IMPERIAL
25 g/1 oz butter
225 g/8 oz long-grain rice
1 small onion, chopped
1 clove garlic, crushed
600–750 ml/1–1¼ pints beef or chicken stock
4 tomatoes, peeled and chopped (optional)
salt and black pepper
50 g/2 oz raisins
2 tablespoons toasted flaked almonds

Illustrated opposite

Heat the butter in a heavy-based frying pan or skillet. Add the rice, onion and garlic and cook, stirring from time to time, until the rice is lightly coloured. Remove from the heat, add the stock, cover and cook for 20 minutes, over medium coals.

Add the tomatoes, if used, and cook for a further 5 minutes, adding a little more stock if the rice seems too dry.

Remove from the heat, season to taste, transfer to a warmed serving dish and sprinkle with the raisins and almonds.

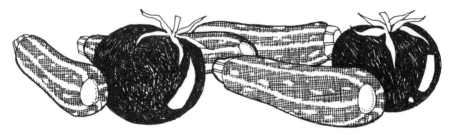

Foiled vegetable medley

Cooking time
30 minutes
Serves 4

METRIC/IMPERIAL
450 g/1 lb courgettes
2 large onions, peeled
4 medium tomatoes, peeled
salt and black pepper
1 clove garlic, chopped
mixed chopped herbs
50 g/2 oz butter

Slice the courgettes and onions thinly and quarter the tomatoes. Mix well together and divide into four equal portions. Place each portion on a square of heavy duty aluminium foil, season to taste, add a little chopped garlic, herbs and butter, and fold the foil to secure the packages.

Cook over medium coals for about 30 minutes, turning once.

Skewered lamb meatballs (see recipe page 52) with outdoor pilaf (see recipe above)

Ratatouille

Cooking time
1 hour
Serves 4-6

METRIC/IMPERIAL
25 g/1 oz butter
3 tablespoons olive oil
2 large onions, thinly sliced
2 cloves garlic, crushed
3 medium aubergines, thinly sliced
1 large green pepper, deseeded and chopped
1 large red pepper, deseeded and chopped
5 medium courgettes, sliced
1 (396-g/14-oz) can tomatoes
1 teaspoon dried basil
1 teaspoon dried rosemary
2 bay leaves
1½ teaspoons salt
¾ teaspoon black pepper
2 tablespoons chopped parsley

Illustrated on page 113

In a large flameproof casserole melt the butter and oil over a moderate heat. Add the onions and garlic and fry, stirring occasionally, for about 5 minutes or until the onions are soft and translucent.

Add the aubergine slices, green and red peppers and courgette slices to the casserole. Fry for 4–5 minutes, shaking the casserole frequently. Add the tomatoes with the can juice, the basil, rosemary, bay leaves and seasoning. Sprinkle over the parsley. Bring to the boil then reduce the heat, cover and simmer for 40–45 minutes until the vegetables are cooked.

Remove from the casserole and serve at once as a vegetable dish, as a basting sauce for meat and poultry or as a starter.

Creamy cabbage

METRIC/IMPERIAL
450 g/1 lb cabbage
6 tablespoons double cream
40 g/1½ oz butter
salt and black pepper

Cooking time
30 minutes
Serves 4

Shred the cabbage finely and wash well. Line a heavy-based casserole with foil. Place the cabbage in the casserole with the cream, butter and seasoning to taste. Cover with a firm fitting lid and cook over medium to low coals for 30 minutes, or until the cabbage is cooked and creamy.

Variations
Red cabbage may be used instead of white and green cabbage during the late summer and early autumn months. Substitute a combination of single cream and chilli sauce or cheese sauce for a more unusual flavour.

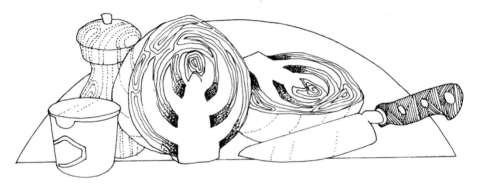

Barbecued baked beans

METRIC/IMPERIAL
100 g/4 oz streaky bacon, rinds removed
25 g/1 oz butter
2 sticks celery
1 medium onion
1 (447-g/15¾-oz) can baked beans
1 tablespoon horseradish sauce
1 teaspoon French mustard

Cooking time
10–12 minutes
Serves 4

Cut the bacon into small pieces and place in a heavy flameproof pan. Heat gently until the fat starts to run. Add the butter and the finely chopped celery and onion. Cook gently, over low coals, until golden.

Add the beans, horseradish sauce and mustard. Cover and heat through over medium coals until the beans are hot. Serve with sausages or hamburgers.

Vegetable kebabs

METRIC/IMPERIAL
6 small potatoes
6 small onions
12 medium mushrooms
2 green peppers
50 g/2 oz butter, melted
½ teaspoon garlic salt
¼ teaspoon black pepper
6 small tomatoes

Cooking time
20 minutes
Serves 6

Peel the potatoes and onions and cook in boiling, salted water until they are barely tender, about 10 minutes. Remove the stems from the mushrooms and wash the caps. Remove the seeds from the peppers and cut into 12 even pieces. Drain the onions and potatoes and alternate on six skewers with the pieces of pepper and mushroom caps. Blend the melted butter, salt and pepper together, and brush the kebabs generously with the mixture. Cook, about 12·5 cm/5 inches above hot coals for 5 minutes. Add a tomato to each skewer, turn the kebabs over and brush with more of the mixture. Continue cooking for about another 5 minutes.

SALADS AND SALAD DRESSINGS

Potato salad

METRIC/IMPERIAL
450 g/1 lb cooked potatoes, peeled and sliced
6 tablespoons mayonnaise
1 tablespoon lemon juice
1 tablespoon olive oil
½ teaspoon salt
½ teaspoon black pepper
2 tablespoons finely chopped chives
4 tablespoons finely chopped leeks

Place three-quarters of the potatoes in a mixing bowl. Pour over the mayonnaise and sprinkle with the lemon juice, oil, salt, pepper and half the chives. Carefully toss until the potatoes are thoroughly coated.

Spoon the mixture into a serving dish. Arrange the remaining potato slices over the top of the salad. Sprinkle with the remaining chives and scatter the leeks around the edge of the dish. Cover and chill for 30 minutes before serving.

Salad mimosa

Serves 4

METRIC/IMPERIAL
2 lettuce hearts, washed and shredded
½ bunch watercress, washed and roughly chopped
2 stalks celery, trimmed and chopped
4½ tablespoons French dressing (see page 88)
2 eggs, hard-boiled and chopped
Garnish
2 oranges, peeled, pith removed and segmented
2 teaspoons olive oil
1 teaspoon white wine vinegar
1 banana, peeled and thinly sliced
1 tablespoon lemon juice
10 green grapes, halved and pipped
1 tablespoon single cream

Combine the lettuce, watercress, celery, French dressing and chopped eggs. Toss until they are all well blended. Transfer to a glass serving dish.

In a small mixing bowl, combine the orange segments, oil and vinegar. In another bowl, combine the banana and lemon juice, and in a third bowl combine the grape halves and cream.

Arrange the fruits and their dressings decoratively over the top of the salad. Serve at once.

Oriental rice salad

Cooking time
10 minutes
Serves 4

METRIC/IMPERIAL
1 small onion, chopped
1 tablespoon oil
2 teaspoons curry powder
1 teaspoon tomato purée
5 tablespoons water
few drops of lemon juice
salt
150 ml/¼ pint mayonnaise
225 g/8 oz long-grain rice, cooked
1 green pepper, deseeded and sliced into rings

Cook the onion in the oil for a few minutes, then add the curry powder and fry for 2–3 minutes. Add the tomato purée, water, lemon juice and salt to taste. Cook for 5 minutes, then strain and cool. Add to the mayonnaise gradually, then mix gently with the hot cooked rice.

Transfer to a warmed serving dish, top with the rings of pepper and serve.

Alternatively, cool the rice and ingredients and serve cold.

Midsummer salad

Cooking time
5 minutes
Serves 6

METRIC/IMPERIAL
2 large slices stale white bread
50 g/2 oz butter
salt
1 clove garlic
1 large Cos lettuce, washed
1 small onion, sliced into thin rings
25 g/1 oz Parmesan cheese
50 g/2 oz button mushrooms, thinly sliced
50 g/2 oz anchovy fillets
6 tablespoons French dressing (see page 88)

Remove the crusts from the bread and cut into 1-cm/½-inch cubes. Fry in the butter until golden brown, drain on absorbent paper and sprinkle with salt.

Rub a large salad bowl with the cut clove of garlic, tear the lettuce into pieces and put into the salad bowl with the remaining salad ingredients. Toss carefully together.

Pour over the French dressing and toss well to coat. Sprinkle with the bread croûtons and serve at once.

Tropical cheese salad

METRIC/IMPERIAL   Serves 6
1 pineapple
175 g/6 oz Cheddar cheese, grated
1 medium dessert apple, cored and sliced
25 g/1 oz walnuts, roughly chopped
25 g/1 oz raisins
4 tablespoons double cream
few drops of Worcestershire sauce
salt and black pepper
few drops of lemon juice
1 tablespoon chopped chives
1 tablespoon chopped parsley
1 lettuce

Cut the pineapple in half lengthways without removing the leafy head. Scoop out the flesh with a sharp knife and cut into bite-sized pieces. Combine the pineapple with the cheese, apple slices, walnuts, raisins, cream, Worcestershire sauce, seasoning to taste, lemon juice, chives and parsley. Pile the mixture back into the pineapple shells. Serve chilled on a bed of lettuce leaves.

Fiesta salad

METRIC/IMPERIAL   Cooking time
2 medium onions, finely sliced   8 minutes
2 medium green peppers, deseeded and coarsely chopped   Serves 6
6 small tomatoes, peeled and chopped
4 rashers streaky bacon, rinds removed
3 tablespoons vinegar
1 teaspoon chilli powder
½ teaspoon salt
few drops of Tabasco sauce
few drops of Worcestershire sauce
1 lettuce

Separate the onion slices and push into rings. Place in a bowl with the peppers and tomatoes.

Fry the bacon in a frying pan until crisp. Remove and drain on absorbent paper. Pour off the bacon drippings, reserving about 2 tablespoons in the pan. Stir in the vinegar, chilli powder, salt, Tabasco and Worcestershire sauce. Heat to boiling. Pour over the salad vegetables and toss lightly.

Wash and dry the lettuce and use to line a salad bowl. Pile the salad ingredients on top and sprinkle with the crumbled bacon. Serve at once.

Cool cheese salad

METRIC/IMPERIAL
150 ml/¼ pint natural yogurt
2 tablespoons mayonnaise
175 g/6 oz Cheddar cheese, cubed
1 carrot, grated
1 red dessert apple, diced
1 red or green pepper, deseeded and chopped
8 stuffed green olives
50 g/2 oz walnuts, roughly chopped
salt and black pepper
1 tablespoon chopped chives
1 lettuce
Garnish
tomato slices

Mix together the yogurt and the mayonnaise with a wooden spoon until smooth. Add the cheese, carrot, apple, pepper, olives, walnuts, seasoning to taste and chives. Mix well to combine.

Line four individual serving dishes with lettuce leaves. Pile the cheese mixture on top. Chill before serving, garnished with the tomato slices.

Walnut, orange and chicory salad

Serves 4

METRIC/IMPERIAL
4 oranges
4 heads chicory, sliced
100 g/4 oz walnuts, chopped
150 ml/¼ pint honey dressing (see page 89)

Peel the oranges, removing as much white pith as possible. Thinly slice into a medium serving dish. Add the chicory and walnuts and pour over the honey dressing. Toss the ingredients together and serve as an accompaniment to barbecued game or poultry.

French dressing

Makes 150 ml/¼ pint

METRIC/IMPERIAL
2 tablespoons red wine vinegar
6 tablespoons olive oil
½ teaspoon salt
¼ teaspoon black pepper
1 clove garlic, crushed (optional)

In a small mixing bowl, beat all the ingredients together with a fork or wire whisk until they are well blended.

Alternatively, put all the ingredients in a screw-topped jar and shake for about 10 seconds. Use as required.

Herb dressing

Makes 300 ml/½ pint

METRIC/IMPERIAL
½ teaspoon chopped chervil
1 teaspoon chopped chives
1 tablespoon chopped parsley
1 teaspoon French mustard
½ teaspoon salt
¼ teaspoon black pepper
1 clove garlic, crushed
225 ml/7½ fl oz olive oil
4 tablespoons tarragon vinegar
2 teaspoons lemon juice

In a small bowl, combine the chervil, chives, parsley, mustard, salt, pepper and garlic with a wooden spoon. Gradually stir in 3 tablespoons of the olive oil. Pour the contents of the bowl into a screw-topped jar. Add the remaining oil, the tarragon vinegar and lemon juice. Firmly screw on the top and shake for 1 minute.

Use as required and store the remainder in the refrigerator until needed.

Honey dressing

Makes 200 ml/7 fl oz

METRIC/IMPERIAL
2 tablespoons clear honey
4 tablespoons lemon juice
6 tablespoons olive oil
$\frac{1}{2}$ teaspoon French mustard
$\frac{1}{4}$ teaspoon salt
$\frac{1}{8}$ teaspoon black pepper

In a small mixing bowl, beat all the ingredients together with a fork or wire whisk, until well blended.

Alternatively, put all the ingredients into a screw-topped jar. Cover the jar and shake for 10 seconds. Use as required.

Onion and paprika dressing

Makes 200 ml/7 fl oz

METRIC/IMPERIAL
6 tablespoons French dressing (see page 88)
1 medium onion, finely chopped
1 tablespoon paprika pepper
$\frac{1}{2}$ teaspoon French mustard
$\frac{1}{2}$ teaspoon sugar
$\frac{1}{2}$ teaspoon black pepper
$4\frac{1}{2}$ tablespoons soured cream

Pour the French dressing into a medium mixing bowl. Add the onion, paprika, mustard, sugar and pepper and beat well with a fork or wire whisk until the ingredients are well blended.

Place the soured cream in another bowl. Gradually add the French dressing mixture to the soured cream, whisking constantly. Serve at once on a mixed salad or pour over freshly cooked vegetables.

Green goddess dressing

Makes 450 ml/¾ pint

METRIC/IMPERIAL
250 ml/8 fl oz mayonnaise
1 teaspoon anchovy essence
3 spring onions, finely chopped
2 tablespoons chopped parsley
2 teaspoons chopped tarragon
1 tablespoon tarragon vinegar
½ teaspoon black pepper
150 ml/¼ pint soured cream

In a medium mixing bowl, combine all the ingredients except the soured cream, and beat well until they are thoroughly blended. Using a metal spoon quickly fold in the soured cream.

Store in the refrigerator and use as required. This dressing makes a delightful addition to mixed salads, or it can be served as a deliciously different filling for jacket potatoes.

Coleslaw dressing

Makes 350 ml/12 fl oz

METRIC/IMPERIAL
300 ml/½ pint mayonnaise
4 tablespoons natural yogurt
1 teaspoon sugar
½ teaspoon salt
1 tablespoon finely grated onion
1 tablespoon finely chopped celery

Blend the mayonnaise with the yogurt, mixing well with a wooden spoon until smooth. Add the remaining dressing ingredients and beat for 1 minute. Use at once.

SAUCES AND MARINADES

A sauce or marinade can make all the difference between an ordinary meal and an unforgettable one. A basting sauce, brushed on the meat as it cooks, adds its own special flavour and keeps the meat juicy and succulent.

A marinade flavours meat and sometimes tenderises it before cooking. Marinate in a tightly covered dish or use a large plastic bag and simply turn the bag to redistribute the marinade. Marinate for several hours in the refrigerator or for at least an hour or two if in a hurry.

Special barbecue sauce

METRIC/IMPERIAL
50 g/2 oz butter
1 onion, finely chopped
1 clove garlic, crushed
2 tablespoons vinegar
150 ml/¼ pint water
1 tablespoon made English mustard
2 tablespoons demerara sugar
1 thick slice lemon
pinch of cayenne pepper
2 tablespoons Worcestershire sauce
6 tablespoons tomato ketchup
2 tablespoons tomato purée
salt and black pepper

Cooking time
25 minutes
Serves 6–8

Melt the butter in a pan and sauté the onion and garlic together gently for about 3 minutes. Stir in the vinegar, water, mustard, sugar, lemon and cayenne. Bring to the boil, cover and simmer for 15 minutes.

Stir in the remaining ingredients, season to taste and continue cooking for a further 5 minutes. Remove the lemon before serving with barbecued meat or poultry.

Orange and lemon barbecue sauce

METRIC/IMPERIAL
2 cloves garlic, crushed
1 large onion, chopped
2–3 tablespoons olive oil
2 teaspoons cornflour
2 tablespoons tomato purée
4 tablespoons demerara sugar
rind and juice of 1 orange
juice of 2 lemons
2 tablespoons Worcestershire sauce
salt and black pepper
150 ml/¼ pint red wine

Cooking time
30 minutes
Serves 6–8

Sauté the garlic and onion in the hot oil until golden in colour. Combine the remaining ingredients well together, then gradually add to the onion, stirring constantly until the sauce thickens. Cover and simmer gently for about 20 minutes. Taste and adjust seasoning if necessary. Strain and serve hot with game, poultry or meat.

Tomato sauce

Makes 300 ml/½ pint

METRIC/IMPERIAL
4 large ripe tomatoes, peeled, *or* **1 (227-g/8-oz) can tomatoes**
4 tablespoons tomato ketchup
1 tablespoon red wine vinegar
2 tablespoons olive oil
few drops of Tabasco sauce
pinch of dry mustard
salt and black pepper

Chop the tomatoes coarsely and mix with the remaining ingredients. Season to taste and serve with barbecued sausages, chops or chicken drumsticks.

Cucumber and yogurt sauce

Serves 4

METRIC/IMPERIAL
300 ml/½ pint natural yogurt
½ large cucumber
salt and black pepper
few drops of Tabasco sauce

Beat the yogurt with a wooden spoon until quite smooth. Peel the cucumber and cut into small dice. Stir into the yogurt. Season to taste with salt, pepper and Tabasco.

Chill before serving with barbecued lamb or chicken.

Sweet 'n' sour sauce

Cooking time
15 minutes
Makes 600 ml/1 pint

METRIC/IMPERIAL
150 ml/¼ pint dry white wine
1½ tablespoons white wine vinegar
1½ tablespoons oil
300 ml/½ pint crushed pineapple (undrained)
1 tablespoon soy sauce
1 teaspoon lemon juice
¼ teaspoon garlic salt
½ teaspoon dry mustard
1½ tablespoons brown sugar
½ small onion, finely chopped (optional)

Combine all the ingredients, mixing well, and simmer in a covered saucepan for about 15 minutes.

Use as a sauce to accompany barbecued chicken or pork, or to baste poultry, pork, lamb, spareribs and fish steaks.

Gooseberry herb sauce

METRIC/IMPERIAL
225 g/8 oz gooseberries, topped and tailed
4½ tablespoons water
2 tablespoons castor sugar
25 g/1 oz butter
1 tablespoon chopped fennel
1 tablespoon chopped parsley

Cooking time
12 minutes
Serves 4

Illustrated on page 37

Place the gooseberries in a small pan with the water, sugar, butter and most of the fennel and parsley. Bring to the boil, reduce the heat and simmer for about 10 minutes.

Remove from the heat, pour into a warmed heatproof dish and sprinkle with the remaining fennel and parsley.

Serve with barbecued mackerel.

Lemon sauce

METRIC/IMPERIAL
2 shallots, finely chopped
50 g/2 oz butter
1 tablespoon flour
300 ml/½ pint dry white wine or cider
salt and black pepper
juice of 1 large lemon
1 lemon, finely sliced
1 tablespoon finely chopped parsley

Cooking time
15 minutes
Makes 300 ml/½ pint

Cook the shallots in the butter until softened but not browned. Add the flour and cook for 1 minute, stirring well. Take off the heat and gradually add the wine or cider, stirring until smooth. Bring to the boil and simmer gently for 5 minutes. Season to taste with the salt and pepper, add the lemon juice and sliced lemon and finally the chopped parsley.

Serve hot with barbecued fish or chicken.

Onion burgers (see recipe page 49) and bacon-wrapped
sausages (see recipe page 57)

Mustard sauce

Cooking time
5–6 minutes
Makes 450 ml/¾ pint

METRIC/IMPERIAL
40 g/1½ oz butter
25 g/1 oz flour
450 ml/¾ pint milk
salt and pepper
1 tablespoon dry mustard
1 tablespoon wine vinegar
1 teaspoon castor sugar

Melt 25 g/1 oz of the butter in a pan, stir in the flour and cook for 1 minute. Gradually add the milk, beating well until the sauce is smooth. Bring to the boil and simmer for 2–3 minutes. Season to taste.

Blend the mustard powder with the vinegar and stir into the sauce. Add the sugar. Check seasoning and stir in the remaining butter.

Serve mustard sauce with barbecued beef, mackerel, sausages and steaks.

Horseradish sauce

Makes 175 ml/6 fl oz

METRIC/IMPERIAL
150 ml/¼ pint double cream
1 tablespoon lemon juice
1 teaspoon grated horseradish
2 teaspoons Worcestershire sauce
2 spring onions, finely chopped

Mix together the double cream and lemon juice. Blend in the remaining ingredients. Allow to stand for at least 1 hour before serving with barbecued steaks and hamburgers or as a topping for baked jacket potatoes.

Skewered rabbit with mustard (see recipe page 60)

Seafood sauce

Makes 175 ml/6 fl oz

METRIC/IMPERIAL
6 tablespoons thick mayonnaise
1 tablespoon tomato purée
2 tablespoons lemon juice
1 tablespoon Worcestershire sauce
1 teaspoon grated lemon rind
1 teaspoon finely chopped onion
2 teaspoons chopped parsley
salt and black pepper

Blend all the ingredients together with a wooden spoon until smooth and well mixed. Place in the refrigerator and chill for at least 1 hour before serving.

Serve with barbecued shellfish, salmon and tuna.

Basic barbecue marinade

Makes 150 ml/¼ pint

METRIC/IMPERIAL
3 tablespoons dry sherry
3 tablespoons soy sauce
3 tablespoons salad oil
1 teaspoon Worcestershire sauce
1 clove garlic, crushed or **1 teaspoon garlic powder**
black pepper

Combine all the ingredients together with a fork or wire whisk to thoroughly blend. Pour the marinade over the food and leave in the refrigerator, turning from time to time, until required.

This marinade can be used for meat, poultry or fish. Steaks will need 3–5 hours, depending upon their thickness, roasts 24–48 hours, depending upon their size, poultry 2 hours and fish 1½–2 hours.

Any remaining marinade can be used as a basting sauce.

Chilli marinade

Makes 300 ml/½ pint

METRIC/IMPERIAL
1 teaspoon chilli powder
1 teaspoon celery salt
2 tablespoons soft brown sugar
2 tablespoons wine or tarragon vinegar
2 tablespoons Worcestershire sauce
3 tablespoons tomato ketchup
150 ml/¼ pint beef stock or water
few drops of Tabasco sauce

Combine all the ingredients together with a fork or wire whisk to thoroughly blend. Pour over the food and leave in the refrigerator, turning from time to time, until required.

Use this marinade for poultry, steaks, spareribs, chops and roasts.

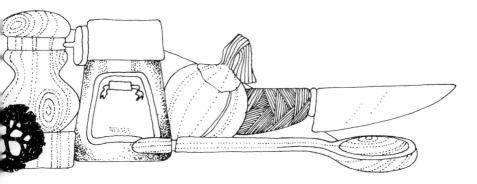

Honey-orange marinade

Makes 900 ml/1½ pints

METRIC/IMPERIAL
6 tablespoons honey
6 tablespoons soy sauce
300 ml/½ pint orange juice
3 tablespoons water
300 ml/½ pint dry white wine
1 teaspoon dry mustard
1 teaspoon paprika pepper
¼ teaspoon ground allspice
1 clove garlic, crushed
few drops of Tabasco sauce (optional)

Combine all the ingredients together with a fork or wire whisk to thoroughly blend. Leave to stand for 1 hour before using to marinate spareribs, chicken or ham steaks. Any remaining marinade can be used to baste the meat during cooking.

Teriyaki marinade

Makes 150 ml/¼ pint

METRIC/IMPERIAL
1½ tablespoons honey
1½ tablespoons salad oil
4 tablespoons soy sauce
¾ tablespoon dry red wine
1 teaspoon grated root ginger
1 clove garlic, crushed

Combine all the ingredients together with a fork or wire whisk until thoroughly blended. Pour over the food and leave in the refrigerator until required.

Use this marinade for poultry, beef, spareribs and fish, and as a basting sauce for the same. Chicken or spareribs should be marinated for 4–8 hours, beef for 8 hours and fish for 2–4 hours.

Seafare marinade

Makes 175 ml/6 fl oz

METRIC/IMPERIAL
150 ml/¼ pint dry white wine
3 tablespoons oil
1 teaspoon paprika pepper
½ teaspoon salt
⅛ teaspoon pepper
1 teaspoon sugar
¾ teaspoon finely chopped parsley

Mix all of the ingredients together to combine well. Use to marinate any seafood or fish before grilling.

Sufficient to marinate 900 g/2 lb of fish.

RELISHES AND CHUTNEYS

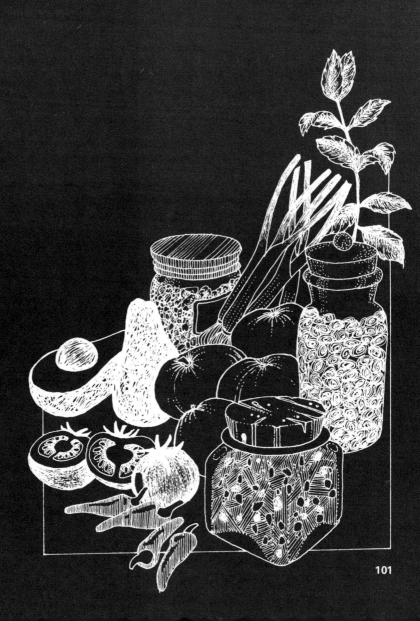

Pepper relish

METRIC/IMPERIAL
6 medium red peppers
8 red or green chillies
450 g/1 lb tomatoes
225 g/8 oz onions
225 g/8 oz cooking apples
2 teaspoons salt
450 ml/¾ pint brown malt vinegar
225 g/8 oz granulated sugar

Cooking time
35–50 minutes
Makes 1·25 kg/2½ lb

Remove the core and seeds from the peppers and chillies. Cut the peppers into quarters. Peel the tomatoes and peel and quarter the onions and the cooking apples.

Coarsely mince the ingredients together. Place in a heavy-based pan with the remaining ingredients. Bring to the boil, reduce the heat and simmer until thick, about 30–45 minutes. Cool, pot and cover.

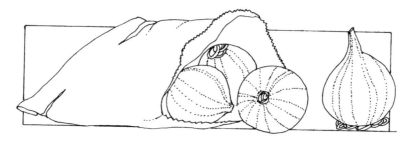

Corn relish

METRIC/IMPERIAL
1 red pepper
1 medium onion
100 g/4 oz celery
450 g/1 lb fresh, canned or thawed frozen sweetcorn
225 g/8 oz granulated sugar
600 ml/1 pint white malt vinegar
2 teaspoons salt
2 teaspoons dry mustard

Cooking time
25–35 minutes
Makes 900 g/2 lb

Remove the core and seeds from the pepper and cut into quarters. Peel and quarter the onion. Pass the pepper, onion, celery and three-quarters of the sweetcorn through a mincer. Place in a heavy-based saucepan with the remaining sweetcorn and ingredients. Bring to the boil, reduce the heat and simmer for 20–30 minutes, until thick. Cool, pot and cover.

Cucumber relish

Cooking time
20–30 minutes
Makes 2 kg/4½ lb

METRIC/IMPERIAL
2 large cucumbers
1 head celery
1 large red pepper
1 large green pepper
450 g/1 lb onions
2 spring onions
900 ml/1½ pints white malt vinegar
1 teaspoon curry powder
1 teaspoon dry mustard
½ teaspoon cayenne pepper
½ teaspoon paprika pepper
½ teaspoon ground ginger
450 g/1 lb granulated sugar

Illustrated on page 37

Wash the cucumbers and cut into short lengths. Scrub the celery and trim. Discard the core and seeds from the peppers and cut into quarters. Peel and quarter the onions. Chop the spring onions. Pass all the prepared ingredients through a mincer.

Put the vinegar in a heavy-based saucepan with the spices. Bring to the boil. Add the minced ingredients and sugar and bring back to the boil. Simmer for 20–30 minutes until thick. Cool, pot and cover.

Mint relish

Cooking time
20–30 minutes
Makes 2·25 kg/5 lb

METRIC/IMPERIAL
900 g/2 lb cooking apples
450 g/1 lb onions
225 g/8 oz tomatoes
225 g/8 oz small sprigs of mint
100 g/4 oz seedless raisins
1 teaspoon dry mustard
2 teaspoons salt
½ teaspoon cayenne pepper
600 ml/1 pint brown malt vinegar
225 g/8 oz soft brown sugar

Peel, core and chop the apples roughly. Peel and chop the onions. Peel, deseed and roughly chop the tomatoes. Chop the mint leaves and raisins finely.

Place all the ingredients in a heavy-based saucepan. Bring to the boil, stirring, then simmer, uncovered, until the mixture has a thick consistency, about 20–30 minutes. Cool, pot and cover.

Avocado relish

METRIC/IMPERIAL
2 avocados
juice of ½ lemon
225 g/8 oz tomatoes
1 bunch spring onions
black pepper
Dressing
2 tablespoons oil
½ tablespoon lime juice
½ tablespoon lemon juice

Peel the avocados and cut the flesh into small dice. Sprinkle with the lemon juice. Peel and chop the tomatoes, discarding seeds and juice, and add to the avocado. Trim and finely chop the spring onions. Mix with the avocado and tomato mixture. Add black pepper to taste.

Make the dressing by combining the oil, lime and lemon juice together. Pour over the avocado and tomato mixture. Chill before serving as an accompaniment to any chicken or dry fish dish.

Instant chutney

Cooking time
8 minutes
Makes 450 g/1 lb

METRIC/IMPERIAL
1 dessert apple
1 medium onion
3 medium tomatoes
2 stalks celery
1 red pepper
1 tablespoon chopped mint
1 tablespoon horseradish sauce
1 clove garlic, minced
25 g/1 oz sugar
2 tablespoons vinegar
1 teaspoon salt
black pepper

Peel, core and finely grate the apple and onion. Peel the tomatoes and roughly chop. Scrub and finely chop the celery. Core and deseed the pepper and cut into small dice. Place with the remaining ingredients in a medium saucepan and bring to the boil. Reduce the heat, cover and simmer for 5 minutes.

Serve hot or cold with barbecued steak, chops, kebabs, sausages and spareribs.

SAVOURY BUTTERS

Garlic butter

Cream 100 g/4 oz butter with 3 finely minced cloves of garlic. Cover and place in the refrigerator until required.

Garlic butter can be used on seafood, grilled lamb chops, beef steaks, hot French bread or jacket potatoes.

Lemon butter

Cream 100 g/4 oz softened butter with 2 tablespoons lemon juice and 1 teaspoon finely grated lemon rind.

Lemon butter tastes delicious spread on seafood, poultry and vegetables, or it can be melted and used as a basting sauce for the same.

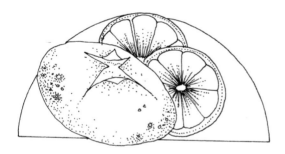

Herb butter

Cream 100 g/4 oz softened butter with $\frac{1}{2}$ teaspoon each finely chopped tarragon and rosemary, 1 tablespoon finely chopped chives, $\frac{3}{4}$ teaspoon minced parsley and salt and pepper to taste. Cover and keep in the refrigerator until required.

Herb butter can be used on cooked vegetables, poultry, seafood and barbecued fish.

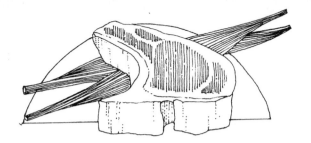

Shallot butter

Lightly sauté 2 tablespoons chopped shallots in $1\frac{1}{2}$ tablespoons butter for about 5 minutes. Combine with $\frac{1}{2}$ teaspoon lemon juice and 100 g/4 oz softened butter.

Serve on seafood, cooked vegetables and chops or use to baste barbecued chicken pieces.

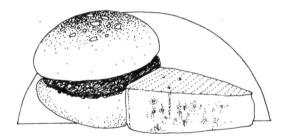

Danish Blue butter

Combine 100 g/4 oz butter with 100 g/4 oz crumbled Danish Blue cheese, $\frac{1}{4}$ teaspoon paprika pepper and 2 tablespoons double cream. Beat until light and fluffy. Cover and keep in the refrigerator until required.

Danish Blue butter is delicious when melted on steaks or hamburgers or used as a filling for baked jacket potatoes.

Anchovy butter

Cream 100 g/4 oz butter with 1½ tablespoons anchovy paste and ¼ teaspoon lemon juice.

Anchovy butter is particularly suitable for spreading on grilled fish steaks or for serving with most seafoods.

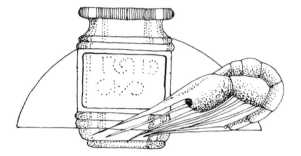

Tarragon butter

Cream 100 g/4 oz softened butter with ½ teaspoon grated lemon rind, 2 teaspoons lemon juice, 1 tablespoon finely chopped parsley, ¼ teaspoon salt and ¼ teaspoon dried tarragon. Beat until light and fluffy. Cover and keep in the refrigerator until required.

Tarragon butter is especially good for seasoning grilled steaks and chicken.

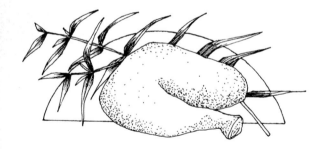

Chef's butter

Combine 100 g/4 oz butter with 2 teaspoons finely chopped parsley, ¼ teaspoon salt, 2 teaspoons lemon juice, ¼ teaspoon dried thyme and a pinch of pepper. Beat until light and fluffy. Cover and keep in the refrigerator until required.

Chef's butter is good for seasoning cooked vegetables and sautéed fish, or an excellent baste for grilled chicken.

ACCOMPANIMENTS

Hot garlic bread

Cooking time
10 minutes
Serves 6

METRIC/IMPERIAL
1 French loaf
100 g/4 oz butter
3 cloves garlic, finely minced
1½ tablespoons finely minced parsley

Thickly slice the French loaf crossways almost to its base along its length.

Cream the butter with the garlic and parsley until thoroughly blended. Spread each segment with a lavish helping of the butter. Wrap the loaf in foil, dull side out, and barbecue over medium coals for about 10 minutes, turning once. Remove from the grill, unwrap, pull the slices apart to free and serve hot.

Barbecued French bread

Cooking time
10 minutes
Serves 6

METRIC/IMPERIAL
1 French loaf
100 g/4 oz savoury butter

Thickly slice a French loaf crossways almost to its base along its length. Spread each cut slice with one of the savoury butters given on pages 106–108. Wrap in aluminium foil, dull side out, and barbecue on the grill, over medium coals, for about 10 minutes, turning two or three times during cooking. During the last 3–4 minutes cooking, open the foil to allow the charcoal flavour to permeate the bread. Remove from the grill and pull each slice apart to serve.

Herb spread

Makes 150 g/5 oz

METRIC/IMPERIAL
100 g/4 oz cream cheese
1 tablespoon mayonnaise
1 teaspoon finely chopped parsley
1 teaspoon finely chopped chives
1 teaspoon finely chopped sorrel leaves
¼ teaspoon salt
⅛ teaspoon white pepper

Combine all the ingredients together in a medium mixing bowl, beating with a wooden spoon until well blended. Place the bowl in the refrigerator and chill for 30 minutes before serving.

Mint and chive spread

METRIC/IMPERIAL
50 g/2 oz unsalted butter
1 tablespoon finely chopped mint
1 tablespoon finely chopped chives
½ teaspoon lemon juice

Combine all the ingredients in a medium mixing bowl, beating with a wooden spoon until well blended. Place the bowl in the refrigerator and chill for 30 minutes before serving.

Hot and cold spread

METRIC/IMPERIAL
100 g/4 oz mild cream cheese
1 tablespoon mayonnaise
1 tablespoon finely chopped radishes
1 tablespoon finely chopped watercress

Combine all the ingredients in a medium mixing bowl, beating with a wooden spoon until well blended. Place in the refrigerator and chill for 30 minutes before serving.

Cheese and herb rolls

METRIC/IMPERIAL
8 bread rolls
175 g/6 oz butter, softened
1 tablespoon finely chopped onion
100 g/4 oz blue cheese or Cheddar cheese, grated
1 teaspoon chopped rosemary
1½ tablespoons chopped parsley
1 teaspoon dried basil

Slice the rolls in half. Combine the remaining ingredients and spread the mixture on the cut sides of each roll. Sandwich the halves back together and wrap securely in aluminium foil. Place on the grill and barbecue over medium coals for 15 minutes, until crisp and hot.

Bacon and onion rolls

METRIC/IMPERIAL
4 rashers streaky bacon
75 g/3 oz butter, softened
1 onion, finely chopped
8 crusty bread rolls

Cooking time
15 minutes
Serves 8

Cut the rind off the bacon, grill until crisp and chop finely. Combine the butter, onion and bacon. Split the rolls and spread the mixture on the cut side of each half. Sandwich the halves together, wrap in aluminium foil and barbecue, over medium coals, for 15 minutes, turning from time to time until crisp and hot.

Honeyed pineapple

METRIC/IMPERIAL
1 medium pineapple
8 tablespoons honey

Cooking time
20 minutes
Serves 8

Remove the top from the pineapple and cut into eight slices. Remove the centre core. Place each slice on a double thickness of aluminium foil and spread a tablespoon of the honey over the fruit. Allow to stand for 10–15 minutes.

Wrap the edges of the foil securely to completely enclose the fruit and barbecue on the grill, over medium coals, for about 20 minutes, turning once during cooking.

Honeyed pineapple makes a delicious garnish for pork chops, spareribs or gammon.

Grilled sardines (see recipe page 62) and ratatouille (see recipe page 80)
Overleaf: Foil-wrapped pork chops and grilled mushrooms

Spiced apples

METRIC/IMPERIAL
6 medium cooking apples
100 g/4 oz brown sugar
2 teaspoons ground cinnamon
40 g/1½ oz walnuts, finely chopped
40 g/1½ oz raisins, finely chopped
25 g/1 oz butter
whipped cream or ice cream

Cooking time
25–50 minutes
Serves 6

Wash and core the apples. Place each on a piece of doubled aluminium foil. Combine the brown sugar, cinnamon, walnuts and raisins, and fill the centres of the apples with the mixture. Top each apple with a little of the butter and secure the edges of the foil firmly to cover. Barbecue on the grill, over medium coals, for about 40–50 minutes, or for 25–30 minutes directly on the coals.

Serve topped with whipped cream or ice cream.

Barbados oranges

METRIC/IMPERIAL
6 oranges
6 tablespoons brown sugar
ground cinnamon
6 tablespoons rum
25 g/1 oz butter
whipped cream

Cooking time
15–20 minutes
Serves 6

Peel the oranges, removing the pith, and divide into segments. Place each portion on a double thickness of aluminium foil. Sprinkle each with a tablespoon of brown sugar, a pinch of cinnamon and a tablespoon of rum. Dot the segments with butter and wrap the edges of the foil to seal. Barbecue on the grill, over medium coals, for about 15–20 minutes.

Remove from the heat and serve hot, topped with whipped cream.

Grilled golden peaches

METRIC/IMPERIAL
12 peach halves (fresh or canned)
100 g/4 oz butter
3 tablespoons sweet sherry or rum
whipped cream or ice cream
few chopped almonds

Cooking time
15 minutes
Serves 6

For each serving place two peach halves, cut side down, on a double thickness of aluminium foil. Turn the edges of the foil up slightly to enclose the peaches. Soften the butter, spread a little over the peach halves and barbecue over hot coals for about 5 minutes.

Mix the sherry or rum into the remaining butter, turn the warmed peaches over and spoon the flavoured butter into the cavities. Barbecue for a further 8–10 minutes.

Serve hot, topped with whipped cream or ice cream and a few chopped almonds.

Fruit kebabs with honey-lemon sauce

METRIC/IMPERIAL
Choose from:
peach halves
pear halves
apple chunks
red and green maraschino cherries
pineapple cubes
stuffed dates
orange slices
Sauce
100 g/4 oz honey
1½ tablespoons lemon juice

Cooking time
5 minutes

The easiest of desserts; prepare a selection of fresh and canned fruits and leave guests to assemble their own choice of fruits and grill to their liking.

Cut a variety of the above fruits into uniform pieces. Thread the fruit on to long skewers.

Prepare the sauce by blending together the honey and lemon. Liberally brush over the fruit kebabs. Grill over medium coals until hot, about 5 minutes. Serve hot with any remaining sauce.

Tipsy trifle

Serves 6

METRIC/IMPERIAL
6 trifle sponge cakes, each sliced into 2 layers
3 tablespoons orange-flavoured liqueur
2 tablespoons fresh orange juice
275 g/10 oz sugar
300 ml/$\frac{1}{2}$ pint custard
4 large oranges, peeled, pith removed and thinly sliced
150 ml/$\frac{1}{4}$ pint double cream, whipped

Place the sponge slices in one layer in a large dish. Sprinkle over the liqueur and orange juice and set aside for 30 minutes, until all the liquid has been absorbed.

In a heavy-based saucepan, dissolve the sugar over a low heat, shaking the pan occasionally. Increase the heat to moderate and boil the syrup, shaking the pan occasionally, until it turns a rich golden brown. Remove from the heat and place the saucepan in a bowl of hot water to keep the caramel warm.

Arrange one-third of the soaked orange sponge slices in a medium glass serving dish. Spoon over one-third of the custard, smoothing it evenly with the back of the spoon. Lay one-third of the orange slices over the custard to cover it completely. Trickle over one-third of the caramel in a thin stream.

Continue making layers in the same way, ending with a layer of caramel-coated orange slices. Place the trifle in the refrigerator and chill for 2 hours.

Fill a piping bag, fitted with a star-shaped nozzle, with the whipped cream. Remove the trifle from the refrigerator and pipe the cream over the top in decorative swirls. Serve chilled.

Chocolate banana splits

Cooking time
10 minutes
Serves 6

METRIC/IMPERIAL
6 firm bananas
175 g/6 oz plain chocolate, cut into small chips
18 marshmallows, cut into quarters

Peel the bananas and cut a wedge out along their lengths, about 1-cm/$\frac{1}{2}$-inch wide and deep. Fill the cavity in each banana with chocolate chips and top with marshmallow pieces. Press the banana wedge back into place and lay each on a piece of aluminium foil. Wrap the edges of the foil securely and barbecue on the grill, over hot coals, for about 10 minutes.

Remove from the heat and serve.

Mocha mousse

Serves 4

METRIC/IMPERIAL
100 g/4 oz plain cooking chocolate
4 tablespoons strong black coffee
4 eggs, separated
150 g/5 oz light brown sugar
Decoration
whipped cream
grated chocolate curls

In a small heavy-based saucepan melt the chocolate in the coffee over a low heat. As soon as the chocolate has melted, remove the pan from the heat and set aside to cool for 10 minutes.

In a large mixing bowl, beat the egg yolks and sugar together with a wire whisk until the mixture is pale and thick. Beat in the cooled chocolate and coffee mixture.

In a medium mixing bowl, whisk the egg whites until very stiff. With a metal spoon fold the egg whites into the chocolate mixture until completely blended. Spoon the mousse into four individual serving dishes. Chill and allow to set before decorating with swirls of whipped cream and chocolate curls.

Fresh lime mousse

Serves 6

METRIC/IMPERIAL
3 eggs, separated
100 g/4 oz castor sugar
finely grated rind and juice of 2 limes
3 teaspoons powdered gelatine
6 tablespoons double cream
Decoration
whipped cream
lime slices

Place the egg yolks in a deep bowl with the castor sugar and grated rind of the limes. Whisk until thick and mousse-like.

Meanwhile, soften the gelatine in a small bowl in the lime juice. Dissolve by standing the bowl in a pan of gently simmering water.

Whip the cream until lightly thick and fold through the mousse with the dissolved gelatine. Lastly fold in the stiffly beaten egg whites and turn into six individual dishes. Refrigerate until firm then decorate with swirls of whipped cream and twists of lime.

Raspberry pavlova

METRIC/IMPERIAL
3 egg whites
175 g/6 oz castor sugar
½ teaspoon vanilla essence
½ teaspoon vinegar
2 teaspoons cornflour
300 ml/½ pint double cream, whipped
450 g/1 lb fresh or frozen raspberries

Cooking time
1 hour
Serves 6

Whisk the egg whites until stiff. Gradually add the sugar, whisking until the mixture is thick and glossy. Whisk in the vanilla, vinegar and cornflour.

Mark out a 20-cm/8-inch circle on a piece of non-stick baking paper. Place on a baking tray. Spoon the mixture within this circle, building it up around the edges. Bake in a cool oven (140°C, 275°F, Gas Mark 1) for 50–60 minutes, until the meringue is crisp on the outside. Cool and carefully remove the paper.

Fill the centre of the pavlova with two-thirds of the whipped cream. Place the remaining cream in a piping bag fitted with a star-shaped nozzle. Pipe swirls of cream around the edge of the pavlova and decorate with the raspberries. Any remaining raspberries may be piled in the centre of the pavlova.

Honeydew melon with blackcurrant iced mousse

METRIC/IMPERIAL
300 ml/½ pint blackcurrant juice
150 ml/¼ pint water
50 g/2 oz sugar
grated rind and juice of 1 lemon
15 g/½ oz powdered gelatine, dissolved in 2 tablespoons hot water
1 egg white
1 large honeydew melon

Cooking time
5 minutes
Serves 6

Turn the thermostat of the refrigerator to its coldest setting.

In a saucepan, combine the blackcurrant juice, water, sugar and lemon rind. Bring to the boil over a moderately high heat and boil for 4 minutes. Remove the pan from the heat and stir in the lemon juice and dissolved gelatine. Pour the mixture through a strainer into an ice-cube or freezer tray. Place in the ice-making compartment of the refrigerator and chill for 30 minutes.

In a small bowl, whisk the egg white until stiff. Whisk the

chilled blackcurrant mixture into the egg white. Spoon back into the ice-cube tray and freeze for a further hour.

Remove from the refrigerator and turn into a mixing bowl. Whisk for 1 minute. Return to the ice-making compartment and freeze for 4 hours.

With a sharp knife, slice the melon crossways into six slices. Scoop out the seeds and place the slices on individual plates. Spoon the mousse into the centre of each piece. Serve at once.

Meringues Chantilly

METRIC/IMPERIAL
Meringues
4 egg whites
225 g/8 oz plus 1 teaspoon castor sugar
Crème Chantilly
300 ml/½ pint double cream
2 teaspoons castor sugar
½ teaspoon vanilla essence

Cooking time
1½ hours
Serves 6

Preheat the oven to cool (140°C, 275°F, Gas Mark 1). Line two baking trays with non-stick silicone paper and set aside.

In a large mixing bowl, whisk the egg whites until they form stiff peaks. Add four teaspoons of the sugar and continue whisking for 1 minute. With a metal spoon, quickly and carefully fold all but 1 teaspoon of the sugar into the egg whites.

Spoon or pipe the mixture into twelve mounds or swirls on the baking trays. Sprinkle with the remaining sugar. Place in the oven and bake the meringues for 1 hour, changing the trays around halfway through baking, or until firm and lightly beige in colour.

Remove the baking trays from the oven and carefully turn the meringues over. Gently press the centres to make a shallow indentation in each meringue. Return to the oven and bake for a further 30 minutes.

Remove the baking trays from the oven and allow the meringues to cool completely.

In a medium mixing bowl, beat the cream with a wire whisk until it is very thick. Add the sugar and the vanilla essence and continue beating until the cream is stiff.

Sandwich pairs of meringues with the flavoured cream and serve.

Redcurrant cheesecake

Serves 6-8

100 g/4 oz plus 1 teaspoon butter, melted
225 g/8 oz digestive biscuits, crushed
1 teaspoon ground cinnamon
450 g/1 lb cream cheese
50 g/2 oz castor sugar
6 tablespoons single cream
575 g/1¼ lb redcurrants, topped and tailed
15 g/½ oz powdered gelatine, dissolved in 2 tablespoons hot water
300 ml/½ pint double cream
1 egg white, stiffly whisked

Lightly grease a 23-cm/9-inch loose-bottomed cake tin with the teaspoon of butter.

In a medium mixing bowl, combine the crushed biscuits, the remaining melted butter and the cinnamon with a wooden spoon. Line the base of the tin with this mixture, pressing it firmly against the bottom. Set aside.

In a medium mixing bowl, beat the cream cheese and sugar together with a wooden spoon until smooth and creamy. Stir in the single cream and 450 g/1 lb redcurrants. Beat in the dissolved gelatine mixture and spoon the mixture on to the biscuit crust. Place in the refrigerator to chill for 30 minutes, or until set.

Meanwhile, in a large mixing bowl, beat the double cream with a wire whisk until it forms stiff peaks. With a large metal spoon, fold the egg white into this mixture.

Remove the cheesecake from the refrigerator. Spoon the cream mixture on the cheesecake, making swirling patterns with the back of the spoon.

Sprinkle the remaining redcurrants over the cream. Chill and serve.

HOT AND COLD DRINKS

Brandied coffee cream

METRIC/IMPERIAL
100 g/4 oz sugar
5 eggs
3 tablespoons brandy
300 ml/½ pint milk
300 ml/½ pint single cream
600 ml/1 pint strong black coffee
3 tablespoons double cream, stiffly whipped
25 g/1 oz plain or milk chocolate, grated

Cooking time
3–4 minutes
Serves 8

In a large mixing bowl, beat the sugar and eggs together with a fork or wire whisk until well blended. Set aside.

In a large saucepan, heat the brandy, milk, single cream and coffee together over a moderate heat until hot but not boiling. Remove the pan from the heat and gradually pour into the egg and sugar mixture, whisking constantly until the ingredients are well blended.

Pour the brandied coffee into eight heatproof glasses. Top with a little whipped cream and grated chocolate and serve immediately.

Mulled claret

METRIC/IMPERIAL
1·4 litres/2½ pints dry red Bordeaux wine
1 tablespoon finely grated orange rind
1 tablespoon finely grated lemon rind
225 g/8 oz sugar
½ teaspoon ground cloves
½ teaspoon grated nutmeg
300 ml/½ pint brandy

Cooking time
5 minutes
Makes 1·75 litres/3 pints

Put the wine, orange and lemon rinds, sugar, cloves and nutmeg into a stainless steel or enamel saucepan. Place over a moderate heat and bring to the boil, stirring constantly to dissolve the sugar. Remove from the heat and pour the wine mixture into a large punch bowl. Set aside.

In a small saucepan, warm the brandy over a low heat until hot but not boiling. Remove from the heat and pour into the punch bowl. Ignite the punch if liked. When the flames die down, serve the punch in heatproof glasses.

Golden fruit punch

METRIC/IMPERIAL
15 ice cubes
300 ml/½ pint white grape juice
300 ml/½ pint apple juice
600 ml/1 pint pineapple juice
475 ml/16 fl oz dry ginger ale
1 small pineapple, peeled and finely chopped *or*
1 (339-g/12-oz) can pineapple pieces, drained
4 sprigs of borage

Put the ice cubes in a very large jug or punch bowl. Add all the remaining ingredients and stir well to blend. Serve at once.

Citrus ponets

Makes 2 litres/3½ pints

METRIC/IMPERIAL
15 ice cubes
1·4 litres/2½ pints white Rhine wine
150 ml/¼ pint vodka
150 ml/¼ pint soda water
juice of 6 medium oranges
juice of 2 large grapefruit
juice of 1 lemon
1 small pineapple, peeled and finely chopped
100 g/4 oz maraschino cherries

Place the ice cubes in a large punch bowl. Add all the remaining ingredients and mix well to blend. Serve at once.

INDEX